GRAND ENTRÉE
The Birth of the Greatest Show on Earth
1870-1875

by William L. Slout

An Emeritus Enterprise Book
2995 Ladera Road, San Bernardino, California 92405
REISSUED IN THE YEAR 2000

Copyright © 1998 by Stuart Thayer and William L. Slout

All rights reserved.
No part of this book may be reproduced in any form
without the expressed written consent of the publishers.
Printed in the United States of America by Van Volumes, Ltd.

Grand Entrée: the birth of the greatest show on earth, 1870-1875
ISBN 0-8095-0309-3 (cloth). - ISBN 0-8095-1309-9 (pbk.)

An Emeritus Enterprise Book
REISSUED IN THE YEAR 2000

TABLE OF CONTENTS

Introduction	vii
Chapter I - Prelude to Barnum, the Coup and Castello Show, 1870	1
Chapter II - P. T. Barnum's Great Travelling Museum, Menagerie, Caravan and Hippodrome, 1871	15
Chapter III - P. T. Barnum's Travelling Exposition and World's Fair, 1872	33
Chapter IV - P. T. Barnum's Great Museum, Menagerie, Hippodrome and Traveling World's Fair, 1873	47
Chapter V - Formation of P. T. Barnum's Great Roman Hippodrome, 1874	65
Chapter VI - First New York Engagement of Barnum's Roman Hippodrome, 1874	83
Chapter VII - Road Engagements, Barnum's Roman Hippodrome, 1874	101
Chapter VIII - Winter Season, Barnum's Roman Hippodrome, 1874-1875	123
Chapter IX - Final Tour, Barnum's Roman Hippodrome, 1875	135
Conclusions and Speculations	159
The Barnum Route from 1871 through 1875	165
Bibliography	173
Index	177

INTRODUCTION

For over a hundred years "The Greatest Show on Earth" has been the identifying slogan of the organization now known as Ringling Brothers and Barnum & Bailey Circus. Over that period, 1871 to today, the circus has had various titles and managements, but one name has been constant in its history, that of one of its original owners, P. T. Barnum.

Before 1871, Barnum's connection with the circus business was limited. He was engaged by Aaron Turner in 1836 for the Old Columbian Circus as treasurer, secretary, and ticket seller. His only experience in show business had occurred during the previous winter when he exhibited the black woman, Joice Heth, purported to have been the nurse of George Washington. When, within a matter of weeks, his drawing card died, he took on a juggler named Signor Vivalla. On joining the Turner circus, Barnum brought Vivalla with him and enjoyed a piece of his salary. The two remained until their contract expired on October 30.

Barnum's experience in circus management was always within a partnership, the one or more partners being the day to day overseers. In 1851, he organized P. T. Barnum's Asiatic Caravan, Museum and Menagerie, with Seth B. Howes and Sherwood E. Stratton as co-proprietors. Although this was not a circus, it was a tented organization that was operated identical to one. The show was profitable throughout its four-year existence—the first two under the management of Howes, the last two under L. B. Lent's direction.

In 1860, Barnum joined with James M. Nixon to exhibit Grizzly Adams' California Menagerie under canvas at Broadway and Thirteenth Street, New York City. Following the opening on April 30, the Menagerie continued to exhibit until July 7; after which, Adams sold his share to Barnum, who then combined with Nixon to take Cooke's Royal Circus with Old Grizzly Adams California Menagerie on tour through the New England States. Performing variously under the titles of Cooke's Royal Circus, Nixon & Adams, and Cooke & Adams, the show moved through Rhode Island, Massachusetts, and New Hampshire until the end of September.

The Barnum & VanAmburgh Museum and Menagerie went out for the summer of 1867, with P. T. Barnum as its president, Hyatt Frost as director, and Henry Barnum as manager. Again, Barnum was lending his name and influence to the management of others. The show featured Tippo Saib, the largest elephant in the country at this time; also, a fifteen foot giraffe, the only one of its kind on the continent; and a double-humped Bactrian camel, royal Bengal tigers, a white Himalayan Mountain bear, silver-striped hyena, lions, leopards, wolves, sacred cattle, panthers, ibex, performing mules and monkeys, South American deer, tapir, baboons, pelicans, silver pheasants, and much more. The museum was composed of curiosities from Barnum's Museum in New York City.

Barnum's fame, in his time and since, has been such that new biographical material appears with regularity. Authors, with good reason, are fascinated by this complex man. In this one individual is found an essential mixture of buncomb and piety that almost mirrors the national spirit. His interests were many, but the dominant part of his career in the societal memory is as owner of the circus that bears his name. Of the man we know much, of the company he founded, little. This book is an attempt to rectify that lack.

Our narrative extends throughout the years when W. C. Coup and Dan Castello were connected with the Barnum name, having been responsible for bringing it back within the title of a traveling amusement. Chapter I deals with a Coup and Castello association which led to that. Chapters II, III, and IV detail the three successful and innovative years with the P. T. Barnum name first connected to a bona fide circus. Chapters V through IX depict the existence of the Great Roman Hippodrome of 1874 and 1875, to which the Barnum focus unexpectedly switched; and after which the Barnum-Coup-Castello partnership ended.

We are indebted to many people and organizations for supplying material for this book. But most particularly we want to acknowledge the Pfening Archives, Columbus, Ohio; Fred Dahlinger, Jr., and staff at the Robert L. Parkinson Library and Research Center, Circus World Museum, Baraboo, Wisconsin; Lee Bayer and Annie Hopkins at Inter-Library Loan, California State University Library, San Bernardino, California. Portions of this material were previously published in *Bandwagon*, the journal of the Circus Historical Society. We thank the Society for permission to reprint.

Stuart Thayer and William L. Slout

GRAND ENTRÉE

The Birth of the Greatest Show on Earth

I
PRELUDE TO BARNUM,
THE COUP & CASTELLO SHOW, 1870

The physical basis of the original Barnum circus of 1871 was a small Wisconsin show that traveled by boat on the Great Lakes through much of 1870. Its title was Dan Castello's Circus & Egyptian Caravan, and that was its first and only season. It was an unlikely vehicle to spawn a major circus. Its assets were less than twenty wagons and less than fifty horses. There was a quartet of highly trained ring horses and a few camels, and not much else. The whole thing was valued at $30,000 at the conclusion of the 1870 season. This was not an inconsiderable sum, yet when one realizes that the Barnum show of 1871 was framed for something near to $100,000, Coup and Castello's physical contribution seems less important.

What the company did have was the talent and experience of an accomplished performer, and the acumen and executive ability of an ambitious showman. These qualities belonged to Dan Castello and William C. Coup, co-owners of the Castello show. These men, both from Wisconsin, provided the impetus for the first real circus upon which Barnum placed his name.

There is also the quality of audacity to be considered. Before their first season together had ended they had approached Barnum, one of the outstanding showmen of the world, with an offer to become his partners. In the somewhat peripatetic business of circus operation (in 1870 one-third of the shows on the road did not answer the bell in 1871), not even being sure they could survive, they apparently believed they deserved Barnum's attention.

Dan Castello of Racine, and William C. Coup of Delavan had formed a partnership the basis of which mirrored the structure of most of the successful efforts at circus management. One man was to oversee the arena, the other to handle the business end. Castello, himself, was once quoted as saying, "There was always one practical man connected with every circus...."[1] Castello, on his record, was not one for counting money and paying the bills, and he was not alone. To this day performers that are good managers are rare.

Dan Castello was born in Kingston, Ontario in 1832, and raised near Syracuse, New York. His father was a quarryman who worked for a firm named Blood & Cady.[2] Dan seems to have begun his circus career in 1849, but it is not until 1854 that we find reference to him. In that year he moved to Delavan and joined the Mabie brothers' circus as an acrobat.[3] If he had served an apprenticeship in the previous five years, it might have been with the June & Turner Circus, according to an 1873 article in the New York *Mercury*. Apprentices were not generally listed in advertising, even though they appeared in performances.

He was with the Mabie company in 1854 and 1855. The first announcement of his appearing as a clown came in 1856, when he was with the John Robinson Circus. By 1857 he had married, as Frances Castello appeared with him as a rider on Harry Buckley's National Circus, a Delavan company. This union was eventually blessed with a son and a daughter, neither of which became performers. Dan Castello, Jr., was an apprentice who made his ring debut in 1870. It is not known if he was adopted by the Castellos. Mrs. Castello was apparently an entry rider, a performer who appeared in the grand entry only, a task not requiring much talent.

In mid-season of 1857, the Castellos left the Buckley show to join Major Brown's circus, perhaps to stay close to home. It could have had to do with Frances being pregnant. She did not accompany Dan that winter when he performed for Spalding & Rogers in New Orleans. In 1858 Dan joined Satterlee-Bell and Co., which was the Buckley circus of 1857.

In addition to his original designation as an acrobat, Castello had become a leaper, one who launched himself from a springboard over various hurdles, be they men or horses or elephants, whatever the company provided. We mentioned above that he had appeared as a clown. In 1859 he added animal training to his accomplishments by purchasing a bull named Don Juan.

He had appeared only with western circuses to this point, but in 1859 he was hired by Nixon & Co., a large eastern firm, where he was advertised as Pedro Gonzalez presenting Don Juan. Presumably, the bull performed as did a trick horse, mounting pedestals, jumping hurdles, and the like.

Nixon went to England in the fall of 1859, and Castello may have accompanied him. Nixon was interested in hiring acts for his circus, Castello was apparently looking for work. In Boston that year he had acquired a trained buffalo, and he took it and Don Juan with him. He caught on with Hengler's Circus, one of England's largest, and spent part of 1860 touring with it. Charles Dickens, an avid circus-goer, saw Castello at the Alhambra in London that year and wrote, "... he did not jump, he flew."[4] In the latter part of 1860 Castello joined Howes & Cushing's American Circus in Ireland. Injured by an attack by the buffalo, and later while performing a leap, he returned to this country in October, 1860. He appeared with Spalding & Rogers in New York that winter, and aboard the *Floating Palace* in New Orleans after the turn of the year.

His next adventure occurred in early 1861, when he had to leave New Orleans with the rest of Spalding & Rogers' winter show. Pete Conklin, the clown, described the event this way:[5]

> We were showing in New Orleans when war was declared between the North and the South. The confederate government stopped our show ... and ordered all northern people to leave the South. We all got together and organized a company, chartered a small steam boat, and fought and "showed" our way up the river. In order to get out of the country we were compelled to "show" under two flags. The show was run on the commonwealth plan. It was called Dan Castello's Great Show, George W. DeHaven, Mgr.

The fact that this little show, of which no notices have been found, was named after Castello seems to indicate the regard in which his fellow performers held him. His name had not appeared in a circus title prior to this. When the show reached Illinois, DeHaven became the owner and Castello was his clown. His injuries had ended his days as a leaper, and from this point he specialized at clowning and animal training. He worked for DeHaven in 1862, and their relationship became a sour one, as Castello avoided the man from then on.

In Fairplay, Wisconsin in 1863, Castello and a lead miner named Richard VanValkenberg framed the Castello & VanVleck's Mammoth Circus. Don Juan, the bull, was a part of this, as was Frances Castello. It was a successful season, according to John Glenroy, but when they reached St. Louis in October, VanValkenburg invited DeHaven into the firm, and Castello left. This indicates that it was Van Valkenburg's money that had backed the company.

Dan Castello

In 1864 Castello became his own man, framing Dan Castello's Own Great Show in St. Paul Minnesota. Chartering the steamboat *Jeannette Roberts* he guided it down the Mississippi and up and down the Ohio. In the fall he spent two weeks in Memphis, and then descended the Mississippi to take advantage of the presence of the Union Army on the lower river. The circus remained close to this audience until spring. In 1865 the route was an upriver journey to Nashville. Here, Castello combined his show with one owned by Seth B. Howes, and managed by Howes' nephew, Egbert.

Seth B. Howes, of Brewster, New York, was a leading circus impresario in the 1860's. His Howe's Great European Circus was the largest show touring in 1865. It had reorganized for a summer tour in Nashville, and left surplus equipment there. It was this gear that was combined with Castello's to form the Howes & Castello's Great Circus, a partnership that lasted until January, 1866.

With the end of the Howes-Castello firm, James M. Nixon stepped in to become Castello's partner, buying the Howes' equipment and leasing some of its animals. The latter were principally four lions under the tutelage of trainer Elijah Lengel, which proved to be the leading attraction of the program for 1867. The show was a success, but Castello's contribution came in for some criticism. One reviewer said of him, "Dan Castello plays clown sometimes, but he never ought to."

The partners arranged to have a menagerie and a museum for 1868. VanAmburgh & Co., the largest traveling menagerie of the day, had not only their own caravan, but a second one which they leased to circus proprietors. This provided an inexpensive system by which circus owners could add to the size of their company. We say inexpensive even though VanAmburgh & Co. might charge as much as 25% of receipts. Buying the animals would be much more costly. What the arrangement was for leasing a museum from Barnum we have no knowledge. Since the names of the owners went with the leases, Castello and Nixon's 1867 show was titled Barnum's Museum Collection & VanAmburgh's Great Menagerie in conjunction with Dan Castello's Great Show. The season ended in February 1868 in Washington, D.C., the winter quarters were established in Frederick, Maryland, and the Barnum and VanAmburgh properties went elsewhere.

When the circus emerged from Frederick in April 1868, and opened its season in Wheeling, West Virginia, it was called Castello, Howes & Nixon, Egbert Howes again joining up, this time as treasurer, and assumedly the money man. If the division of ownership was as it was in 1869, Castello had fifty percent, and Howes and Nixon each twenty-five. They went as far west as Kansas City, and ended the season in Mobile, Alabama, where they wintered.

The 1869 season began with a route across the South to Savannah, from where they went north to Virginia and west to Tennessee, and then out to Kansas. They reached Omaha just as the Union Pacific Railroad was finishing its track to California. At Nixon's urging the show (ten cages, a bandwagon, two elephants and two camels) was loaded on the railroad to proceed across the plains, the first circus in history to go coast to coast in a single season. Castello later said they netted $1,000 a day for thirty-one straight days. Much of the circus was sold in California. His half of the profits amounted to $60,000.[6]

Castello's career, though briefly recited here, has to be considered a successful one, nineteen years to the point where he got with Coup to plan their 1870 venture.

William Cameron Coup was born in Mt. Pleasant, Indiana, in 1837. One of six children of a tavern owner, he left a job in a printing office in 1852 to join P. T. Barnum's Caravan, a traveling museum and menagerie that existed from 1851 to 1854. This was his introduction to the exhibition business; his first job was apparently as a roustabout. He tells in his autobiography of being with the L. G. Butler circus in the 1850's. This could have been anytime between 1853 and 1856, as Butler was on the road all those years. Conceivably, it could have been all of them. We find Coup again in the winter of 1860, conducting a wax figure show in the Caribbean. In 1861 he joined the Mabie aggregation as manager of the sideshow with Harry Buckley. This occupied him through 1865, when he switched to Yankee Robinson's circus. Here again he managed the sideshow and was assistant manager of the circus. This was as close to actually operating a circus that he reached; his effort with Castello was his first incursion in managing an entire circus. Yet Barnum said of him: "He was a capital showman and a man of good judgment, integrity, and excellent executive ability."[7]

Apparently Mrs. Coup prevailed upon her husband to abandon show life after the 1869 season, and he bought a farm in Delavan and invested in a local bank. But this hiatus was of very short duration. Coup's obituary in the New York *Clipper* stated that he met Castello on the street in Chicago. It would seem most likely that Coup was the instigator of their talks, since Castello was the better-known personality. In any event, they agreed to organize a circus for 1870.

Coup had the idea of putting their company on a Great Lakes steamer, more properly a "propeller." Floating circuses were no rarity in nineteenth century America; at least two companies had appeared in propellers on Lake Michigan in the late 1860's. So much of the national traffic moved by water it was logical that entertainers would do the same. Because there was no great investment in horses and wagons, and because water transport was a tenth the cost of overland travel, the appeal is obvious. Most of this movement was on the great rivers, where the preponderance of western population lived. The Great Lakes had been largely ignored for this reason. Lake Erie, from Buffalo to Detroit, was a fairly busy circus route, as were some cross-lake avenues on Lake Ontario, but the others, Huron, Michigan, and especially Superior were mostly barren of such travel.

The partners must have realized that the demand for timber and iron during the Civil War had created population growth in both Michigan and Wisconsin. There were good-sized towns in Michigan's Upper Peninsula, for example, that hadn't existed ten years before. Those that had were swelled by the wartime boom. They would be visiting towns where a circus would be a great novelty. Castello and his partners had done the same thing in Colorado and Utah in 1869, and made money doing it. Showmen were constantly seeking new territory, places where circuses had not or had seldom visited.[8]

Castello trained the horse acts in Racine. He owned several highly trained trick horses, that is, ones that performed without a rider. They were Czar and Floating Cloud and January, to which he added a stallion named Senator. January was apparently a pony, though Castello, who invented the "January" act, had also used mules. A January act was one in which the clown entered the ring with the pony and sold it to the ringmaster, who subsequently could not get the animal to move. The clown then entered the ring, whispered in the pony's ear, and it thereupon responded. There were variations of all sorts with this basic theme. In addition to the horses, Castello had two comic performing mules, the gist of whose comedy also had to do with obstinacy.

As we said, the complete title of the company was Dan Castello's Great Circus & Egyptian Caravan. The caravan part referred to the eight Bactrian camels that the managers obtained from the pool of animals that the Army was selling for $80 each after an unsuccessful

William Cameron Coup

attempt to use them as substitutes for mules in the southwest. Castello and Coup advertised that they were the first such animals to perform in a circus ring. They were featured in a spectacle entitled "The Halt in the Desert," and as propulsion for the band wagon in the downtown "bally-hoo" that passed for a street parade. The season may have been difficult for the beasts, as early ads read "these are the genuine double-humped Bactrian camels," but later ads said "at least two of them are the genuine double-humped ...," indicating that some had been replaced by the more common dromedaries.

The finale of the program was a burlesque of a Ku Klux Klan initiation, so there is little doubt no southern tour was planned. Castello was ringmaster, clown, horse trainer and co-proprietor, making it truly Dan Castello's circus. Coup was apparently indifferent to having his name in the title; of course he was not known to the general public.

Most of the administrative positions, and much of the labor it would seem, came from Delavan. George Bishop was the manager, and Edward Buckley his assistant. Stephen S. Babcock was the advance agent with W. May Gildersleeve as assistant. It has been written that Coup did not plan to actively involve himself with the day-to-day operation, probably as a sop to his wife, and the appointment of Bishop would seem to bear that out. Coup did, however, handle some aspects of the advance. This is proven by newspaper accounts of his presence.

The show was advertised as "the largest equestrian company ever organized in America," but it fell far short of that. The riders were Dan's wife, Frances Castello, who evoked no copy from reviewers that season; Dan, Jr., an apprentice, who received occasional mention; Philo Nathans, a pad rider of twenty years experience; Estell Nathans, his daughter or apprentice; Frances Donaldson, a *corde volante* or ribbon-jumping rider, who came in for a share of acclaim in reviews; Mlle. Virginie, an unknown, and young John Saunders, an English bareback rider who was undoubtedly the best in the group.

Other artists were Miaco, Hawley & Rivers (Tom Miaco, David Hawley), the trapezists, who were praised as poised and graceful upon occasion. Miaco (Tom Eastlake) had been performing since at least 1852. The Salinyea Brothers, Charles, George and Henry, were ground acrobats, described as mundane acrobats in the advertising, an interesting example of the effect of time on word usage.

It was originally announced that the circus would travel aboard the steamer *Sarah Van Eps,* but the arrangement was not consummated, and the boat actually chartered was the wooden propeller *Benton.* This was a fairly new boat, having been launched at Buffalo in 1867. It was 152 feet long with a beam of twenty-eight feet, and a net weight of 159 tons. In the trade for some years it brought $8,000 in 1881 when it was bought by the Gilchrist Transportation Company of Vermillion, Ohio. Its final owner was W. E. Pierce of Bay City, Michigan. It burned at River Rouge, Michigan in August, 1909. The captain was one John Morrison, well-known on the Lakes because he had been the skipper of the *Hippocampus,* which sank in a storm in 1868 while plying between St. Joseph, Michigan and Chicago.

The size of the boat limited the size of the circus. They carried few, if any, baggage wagons, and no baggage stock to speak of. It is probable that the equipment went from boat to lot to boat again by hired dray. The parade was a circuit of each town by the bandwagon followed by the beautiful ring stock.

On May 18, or thereabouts, the tent was erected in Racine to facilitate rehearsals. It was decided to play two inland dates before boarding the *Benton.* On May 26 they were in Union Grove, and on May 27 in Burlington before returning to Racine for May 28. The trip inland may have been undertaken as a "shake-down" journey. Both performances in Racine were turnaways. Castello was popular in his home town. Little Dan received some notice for his act, and Miaco, Hawley & Rivers were termed "frightful, and yet so graceful."[9]

Sunday, May 29, was spent crossing Lake Michigan to Saint Joseph, Michigan, where they performed on the 30th. On the 31st they moved up to Benton Harbor, and then successively to Grand Rapids on June 3, Muskegon, June 4; Grand Haven, June 9. On June 10 they crossed the lake again, this time to Milwaukee.

The two-day Milwaukee stand was heavily billed, though there was no opposition. In fact, there was no opposition during the whole of the season. Many Wisconsin towns saw but the one circus in 1870.

A writer for the Milwaukee *News* got carried away by the sight of all the lithographs, and waxed eloquent in a tongue-in-cheek art review in which he said, "Active hanging committees stir about seeking broad surfaces which they may convert into National Academies.... A marked preference is shown for large canvasses, great works of art are decidedly the thing just now ... a pointed leaning toward animated nature ... still life is not in vogue." He went on to say that if anyone doubted that the circus had the steeds or the trapezists or the lady riders, he had only to visit the circus to be sure.

Again the houses were large for the June 10 and 11 performances. "It must have been very gratifying to the proprietor," said the *News*. "The desire to present to the public an exhibition free of all vulgarity is a rare ambition in a circus manager."

From Milwaukee the route led north to Port Washington, Sheboygan, Manitowoc, Two Rivers, Kewanee and Ahnepee, all coastal towns. The reviewer in the Manitowoc *Pilot* said "the performance throughout was all that the advertisements and posters presented ... a rare occurrence in these days of high pressure advertising and buncombe show bills." The mules were described as "brilliant in obstinacy," and Johnny Saunders and Frances Donaldson were loudly applauded by the audience.

The circus boat proceeded through the channel at Sturgeon Bay; a show was presented on June 20. Special arrangements were made by the Goodrich Line to bring people down by boat from the northern part of the peninsula on Sunday night, and take them back Tuesday morning, giving them all day Monday at the show grounds. Castello was in indifferent health on this date and scarcely appeared in the ring.

Down Green Bay the route led to the town of the same name for the June 21 performance and then into the Fox River for a stand at DePere. Coup, handling the advance, was complimented by the Green Bay paper as being a gentleman, an encomium that many commentators have made of him.

The next move was north to Duluth and Oconto, and then into Michigan at Menominee. The only natural problem of the entire season occurred here when a storm hit Menominee and blew down the big top. The Escanaba *Tribune* said, "It must have made the camels think of home sweet home." From Menominee the show went to Escanaba and then overland, presumably in hired wagons. Stands were made at Negaunee, Ishpeming, and Marquette on Lake Superior. The *Benton* could have gone on to Sault Ste. Marie, through the locks, and west to pick up the troupe for the run back to the Soo.

They moved down the east coast of Michigan to play at Tawas, Bay City, and East Saginaw. Unfortunately, the then sparsely-populated area had few newspapers, thus reconstructing the path is difficult. Port Huron and its Canadian twin, Sarnia, were visited on July 14 and 15,

BENTON [Courtesy of the Dossin Great Lakes Museum, Detroit, MI.]

and sometime between the 18th and 25th the circus backtracked north since they billed Au Sable for that week.

It must be that they went back up Lake Huron playing small towns in Michigan. There were few villages on the Ontario side in that region. On August 16 they were in Kenosha, Wisconsin, and next day in Waukegan, Illinois. This ended the water-borne phase of the season. The *Benton* deposited them in Racine.

A contract had been made between the circus and two Delavan men to transport the show overland from Racine for sixty days. These men, D. B. Barnes and Harry Buckley, brother of the assistant manager, agreed to furnish forty-two horses and enough wagons for a price of $3,600.

They contracted with Fish Brothers, the well-known Racine wagon-builders, about the first day of August, and the wagons were built in two weeks. Fish Brothers had been organized as Fish & Bull in 1862, and became Fish Bros. in 1864. At the height of its prosperity the firm had 200 employees engaged in the manufacture of buggies and farm wagons. It was in business on State Street until World War I.[10] The wagons they provided to Barnes and Buckley were drays, such as delivery men used, a close configuration to farm wagons. Forty-two horses indicates about fourteen wagons. D. B. Barnes sold these horses to the Barnum circus in 1871 for $3,900. He was later a banker in Delavan; he must have been a very good one.

If Coup approached P. T. Barnum in person to advance the idea of the great showman joining him and Castello in a show for 1871, this period of change from boat to wagon would have been a good time to do so. There is no evidence as to how the proposition was offered. W. Gordon Yadon has written that Coup wrote the old showman at least twice. We only know that Barnum agreed to the scheme by October 8, the date of an extant letter accepting the idea.

The circus went overland to a near-blowdown in Columbus on August 25. Rain had threatened all day, and the tent was about half-full for the evening performance when a man rushed in and announced that a hurricane was approaching. The canvas was lowered so quickly that some people were caught under it. A tremendous electrical storm followed, however there were no injuries or property damage.

For the stand at Fond du Lac on August 27, and thereafter, the company used a fancy newspaper cut of a band wagon. Several newspapers subsequently alluded to the beauty of the vehicle, indicating that something changed at that point. The cut, later used by Coup on the Barnum circus, was of the Seth Howes' Globe telescoper, which they surely didn't have. He offered a light band wagon for sale in 1871; the Barnum show's band wagon was not a light one.

They proceeded through Berlin to Neenah-Menasha and over to Stevens Point by September 9. The performances elicited nothing unusual from reporters. They were in Portage on September 15, Baraboo on the 17th, Reedsburg the 19th, Mauston the 20th, and Sparta the 23rd. LaCrosse, Melrose and Black River Falls followed. Over 4,000 people saw two performances in Black River Falls on September 29.

By October 19, the troupe had reached Winona, Minnesota, and the contract with Barnes and Buckley was ended. Presumably, the show went back to Delavan and into winter quarters on Coup's property.

Dan Castello's Great Circus & Egyptian Caravan had been a success. Coup valued the property at $30,000 at season's end. He was quoted as saying, "Our trip was one of perpetual delight and not a little pecuniary profit." The partners, with Barnum's agreement in hand, set about preparations for the 1871 season.

NOTES

[1] "A Nestor of Clowns," interview of Castello, Syracuse *Standard*, (n.d., n.p.n.).
[2] W. Gordon Yadon, "Daniel A. Castello," p. 3.
[3] George F. Holland, "A Long Lifetime With a Circus," p. 32.
[4] Yadon, *op. cit.*, p. 4.
[5] *Billboard*, May 13, 1911. Conklin misspeaks, as war wasn't declared until April, 1861. The commonwealth plan refers to a cooperative, in which everyone shares expense and income.
[6] Syracuse *Standard, op. cit.*
[7] Arthur H. Saxon, *P. T Barnum*, p. 231.
[8] Fred D. Pfening, III, "The Frontier and the Circus," p. 16.
[9] The known route appears in the appendix. The lengthy list of newspaper sources has been eschewed in favor of brevity. All the Wisconsin and Michigan sources were read at the State Historical Society of Wisconsin, the Michigan Historical Collections, and the Michigan State Library.
[10] Pat Dunn, "Souvenir Tells Own Story of Racine's Past," p. 1.

II
P. T. BARNUM'S GREAT TRAVELLING MUSEUM, MENAGERIE, CARAVAN AND HIPPODROME, 1871

P. T. Barnum wrote his friend Moses Kimball in February 1871, "I thought I had finished the show business (and all others), but just for a flyer, I got it once more." W. C. Coup had contacted him in the fall of 1870, and offered him a percentage of the profits for the use of his name in a circus title. Barnum refused, stating he had no interest in getting back into show business. Coup wrote a second time, saying the old showman could stay in retirement, all they wanted was his name.[1] Dingess relates that Barnum's family was so opposed to his going back into business that when Coup called at the house in Bridgeport, they wouldn't admit him. But Barnum decided that he needed some kind of grand project, and in an oft-reproduced letter of October 8, 1870, Barnum accepted Coup's offer, and Castello and Coup went to Barnum to work on details.

Castello's version of his trip east went like this:[2]

> Coup was in New York, and he wrote to me that he wanted to see me. I did not pay any attention to the letter, but I soon received a telegram to come at once. I did not know what was the matter, and so I told my wife that I was going to Chicago. Well, I went to Chicago, but went on to New York, too. When I got there Coup met me and took me to see Barnum. That was in 1870 and 1871.

Coup and Castello, on the evidence, assumed they would simply apply Barnum's name to their circus. And it is certain that it was the most valuable investment in the new enterprise. Barnum was "famous," he was a "celebrity." In those years, when politicians or soldiers were the best-known public figures—and the ideals held up to children—Barnum and one or two others, Harriet Beecher Stowe and Horace Greeley among them, had achieved what today is readily available, notoriety unaccompanied by any real cultural contribution. Barnum had spent a lot of time and money making his name known, and the chances of success of a circus bearing it were exceeded only by the possibilty of Ulysses S. Grant lending his name to a field show.

The Wisconsin partners soon found out that Barnum was "in for a penny, in for a pound," as he enthusiastically set about lining up museum attractions for the new show. Many, in fact most, commentators denigrate Barnum's ability as a circus proprietor, usually settling for statements that he was ignorant of the process, and giving the palm to Coup as the organizer and actual operator. An important exception to this view is that of Arthur Saxon, author of the definitive biography of the showman, who cites the many contributions Barnum made to the advancement and success of the undertaking.[3] Coup himself, twenty years later, said, "As far as the technical details of the show were concerned, Mr. Barnum was absolutely ignorant, but in its place he possessed an amount of commercial daring and business sagacity that which amply atoned for his other shortcomings."[4] In this regard we can only quote Barnum himself in reply to the question of a journalist, "I'd burst up in a year if I undertook to manage a circus. I don't know anything about the details."[5]

Barnum's major contribution to the actual operation of the company was his invention of the courier, a newspaper-type throwaway that was distributed ahead of the show, and extolled its wonders. In fact, the introduction of this type of advertising was the most important improvement in circus advertising since the introduction of lithographed posters. Like the lithographs, the couriers were broadcast by the millions, and are still used in the business.

"I was to foot the bills," Barnum wrote.[6] But Castello reported that each of the three men put in $60,000.[7] If the statement in the New York *Tribune* of August 19, 1871, is to be believed, the total investment was nearly $500,000. Perhaps Castello's figure was on the order of seed money. If so, Barnum's bills were of some magnitude. The ownership was divided two-thirds to Barnum with Coup and Castello splitting the other third.

George Wood, the New York Museum operator who used Barnum's name, paid the showman three percent of the gross receipts for the privilege. Barnum and Coup had a similar agreement. Coup reported that the season's gross, exclusive of the privileges (i.e. concert, candy and sideshow) was $400,000, so Barnum picked up at least $12,000 from that, about the same amount he received from Wood in a year.

D. B. Barnes and Harry Buckley had provided forty-two horses for the Coup-Castello circus and these were purchased for the 1871 Barnum show for $3,900. The wagons they had pulled were made by Fish Brothers Wagon Company in Racine.

The equipment going from Coup-Castello to the Barnum organization was shipped by rail from Delavan to Bridgeport, Connecticut, in the spring of 1871 and was carried on ten cars. The forty-two horses and ten railroad flats would seem to indicate about fourteen wagons, though it is doubtful that the Castello show needed that many.

In addition to himself as general manager and Castello as equestrian director, Coup hired several Delavan showmen for the season. Ed Buckley (1836-1892) was assistant manager; Luke Tilden (1828-1877) parade supervisor: Washington Smith (1847-1904), six-horse chariot driver; George Madden (1836-1895), clown; Mary Anne Madden (1847-1895), rider; and George Sloman (1832-1904), trapeze performer. Others from Delavan were Harry Buckley, George Bushnell, William Smith, Bob Westendorf, Harriet Buckley, Harry Ambler and Frank Delaney.[8]

Other staff people were W. C. Crum, treasurer; J. J. Justice, contracting agent; J. L. Hutchinson, agent for Barnum's autobiography and later with the advance; W. L. Jukes, in charge of mechanical figures; and Dr. A. C. Berry, veterinary surgeon. There were many others, of course, but these all figured in later seasons with Barnum.

Barnum satisfied himself with appointing the assistant treasurer, his son-in-law, S. H. Hurd. He was there to protect Barnum's interest. Also, Barnum had sole claim to sales of his autobiography, less the value of the free ticket provided with each. The books were sold for one dollar and fifty cents and J. B. Pond, who managed Barnum on the lecture circuit, said they sold in the tens of thousands and that Barnum paid nine cents for them. Add in the privilege money and one can see that Barnum was handsomely rewarded for his mortgages and the use of his name.

The first public announcement of the formation of Barnum's Circus appeared in the New York *Clipper* on February 2, 1871. A month later the receipt of a shipment of imported animals by steamer was reported. This does not correlate in terms of time with Coup's assertion in the Baltimore *Gazette* in an 1878 interview to the effect that they had telegraphed to Europe for wild animals which were shipped on the *Erie*. They were due in New York in fourteen days from Hamburg (probably from Reiche Brothers), but sixty days elapsed before they learned that she had broke her screw and put into St. Thomas. By then the crew had eaten all the animals except the rhinoceros.

"We, however," Coup was quoted, "arranged to purchase a menagerie that had been traveling over the country sinking (i.e. losing) money, but got animals from Europe instead, there being time."

To oppose both is Barnum's statement in his letter to Coup of October 8, 1870, in which he wrote, "Wood will sell all his animals right." Apparently, Wood would not.

Thus we have two menageries coming from Europe, one of which was eaten by hungry sailors; a domestic menagerie and Wood's animals. Whatever the source, the menagerie was finally put on display with twelve camels (some from Coup and Castello), four lions, the rhinoceros, zebras, two elephants (one large, one small), gnus, yaks, elands, tawny and black leopards, kangaroos, white deer, boars, birds, and monkeys. In all, enough beasts to fill thirty cages. A giraffe, purchased abroad, died en route—possibly as lunch—and another was purchased, but we find no proof of its arrival in time for the outdoor season.

The museum attractions were many and show the Barnum hand. Platform acts included Admiral Dot ("smaller than Thumb"), a giant, a bearded lady, an armless girl, and a sleeping woman. Wax figures and mechanical marvels were carried in wagons in those days and one report credits the show with twenty museum vans.[9] Among these were General Moltke, the victor of 1870; Siamese twins; King William of German, again the Franco-Prussian War; a Cardiff giant; Louis Napoleon; a dying Zouave; a mechanical trumpet player and a perpetual motion machine. Most of these seem to have come from Wood.

The existence of twenty museum wagons and our previous statement that there were thirty cages may not mean fifty parade units. It could well be that the thirty cages counted by the New York *Clipper* included the twenty museum wagons. The latter, being paraded closed, could easily be mistaken for cages and the animals we listed would fit nicely into ten dens.

The entire aggregation moved in ninety-five to one hundred wagons[10] pulled by two hundred forty-five horses driven by one hundred seventy-five teamsters. In addition, there were sixty arenic stars and seventy-five other employees. The New York *Times* said it was the largest show of its type ever, and it might well have been true.

Because of the terms of his contract with George Wood, Barnum could not show under his own name in New York City, so the opening date, April 10 to 15, was in Brooklyn. Later, Barnum paid Wood $12,000 to cancel this clause, and the circus went into the American Institute Building at 63rd Street and 3rd Avenue on November 13.[11]

The Brooklyn lot was a new one on Fulton Avenue between Smith and Hoyt Streets near City Hall. It had replaced the lot at Fulton and DeKalb just the year before. Eighteen seventy-one was the first season in which any show used three tents to separate the menagerie, the museum, and the arena. The two circuses that introduced the idea were J. E. Warner's Great Pacific, out of Lansing, Michigan, and Barnum's.[12] There had been separation of the menagerie for several years because of the growth of that department with the larger shows. Museums, or sideshows, however, had not reached such a size, generally speaking, as to require them to be self-tented. Barnum's big top was much larger than the other two tents, but we have found no record of its size. Capacity seating eventually amounted to 9,300 people, though it was 5,000 at season's beginning. This was a round top, the seats being set up on the ground for a distance around the ring and bleacher seats

being behind them. The chairs on the ground, or some of them, composed the reserve seating, the rest the equivalent of today's blues. There was no crowd control inside the big top, as we shall reveal later, so the people in the rear seats often pushed forward in the aisles the better to see and the people in the chairs stood on their seats. Coup gave this state of affairs credit for the introduction—in 1872—of two rings.

In addition to the three public tents, there were either five or eight horse tents, maybe both, dependent on the lot.[13] Each apparently held about thirty head of baggage stock. The ring stock was boarded daily in livery or hotel stables and on the days of long moves, thirty to forty miles, was shipped by rail.

There was also a dining tent and a wagon fitted up to be a cookhouse. While the staff and performers still stayed in hotels, after the time honored custom, the working men were provided with beds on the lot. These were in the form of fold-down bunks in the baggage wagons, twelve bunks to the wagon. While this system, feeding and bedding the help on the lot, was more economical than the old way of putting them up in hotels every night, it was also the only solution for a crew the size of Barnum's. There would not be enough hotel rooms in the average town to house almost three hundred people. Coup once stated that he believed that well-rested men worked better so he saw to it that everyone had a bed on the rail show; he evidently believed this by 1871.

"No Saratogas" was a common warning in hiring ads in trade papers in the 1870s and it referred to the refusal by shows to carry trunks for the personnel. If everyone attached to the company brought a trunk with them, many additional baggage wagons would be required to haul them about. Thus, everyone was limited to satchels of one sort or another for which they had to accept the safety. Coup provided one baggage wagon in which anyone's goods and clothes could be hung and numbered, guarded by a clerk who handed out whatever was requested. It was a check room on wheels.[14]

The canvas crew consisted of twenty-eight men and they could erect the tents in thirty-five minutes. Building the ring and erecting the seats took another forty minutes. The ring was an earthen, banked circle, sloped on the interior side to help give purchase to the horses. It was constructed anew at each stand. Tear-down was measured at twenty-eight minutes. All this dependent, of course, on lot and weather conditions.[14]

In most 1871 stands the Barnum show gave three performances, 11 a.m., 2 p.m. and 8 p.m. There were many times during the season when even these were not enough and the closed ticket wagons would be surrounded by people offering two and three times regular admission for a ticket. There were three ticket wagons in Boston in June and four in Rochester, New York, in September; so one may have been added to handle the rush that became commonplace. The nut was about $2,500 according to several sources indicating that five thousand people at fifty cents a head would handle expenses. Children were admitted for twenty-five cents. Only the smallest towns could not support the show and only in Maine were such towns encountered.

It is doubtful that any previous street parade was as grand as the one presented by P. T. Barnum's Circus in 1871. The thirty wagons (menagerie and museum) that we have mentioned above were all new since Coup-Castello had none. These were highly varnished and some had mechanical figures, their movements geared to the wagon axles, which caught the attention of most observers. One in particular had a large rosebud atop it which opened as the wagon moved, revealing a statue of cupid. These were of American manufacture, according to the *Clipper*, but we do not yet know who made them. There is also a reference to six royal chariots mounted with golden lions, elephants, and tigers.

The two important vehicles in the parade are also still mysteries to us insofar as their origin is concerned. The first of these is the "Chariot of Orpheus," a name used here with some caution. During the 1870 season the Dan Castello Circus acquired a new bandwagon about September 26 in LaCrosse, Wisconsin. It may well have been this wagon. Where it came from and who built it are not known and the Castello show did not advertise it. We know of its existence from editorial comment. If it did not come from the Castello troupe to Barnum then it must have been built for the 1871 show. It was the only bandwagon in the Barnum parade and was pulled by a team of camels, just as the Coup-Castello one was. Its presence is confirmed by heralds, posters and newspaper accounts.

The Exeter, New Hampshire *News-Letter* of July 14 says "the second and less pretensions chariot was drawn by eight horses and several camels." The Rochester *Daily Union* of September 19 puts them at twelve horses and ten camels. The *Clipper* of April 15 refers to ten camels. It is possible that hilly parade routes led to the use of horses in addition to camels.

The *Clipper* called it the "Car of the Muses," which fits its role as bandwagon. It was twelve feet long and eight feet wide with oval mirrors, two to a side, with a carved animal head between them. A knight in armor sat in each corner of the wagon and the band sat in the middle, facing out in all four directions. We suspect that this vehicle was rebuilt for the 1872 season as we cannot believe that an eight-foot wide body could be carried on the small flatcars of that era. There is no record of the wagon after 1873.

The second, and best known, of these parade vehicles was the "Revolving Temple of Juno." This appears to be an English-made wagon.[15] The *Clipper* says so, Barnum says so, and its appearance suggests it. It was surmounted by a throne over which a suspended canopy could, when the wagon body was fully extended, reach at least thirty feet in the air (advertising claimed forty feet). There are references to men with poles being on the wagon to lift telegraph wires out of the way, but in those days wires might sag to within fifteen feet of the street. The throne revolved through a gear arrangement with the axles. In parade, a pretty lady dressed like a queen sat on the throne. It appears that there were two telescoping sections, the larger being mounted with mirrors ten feet long and five feet wide divided into four plates. Inside this was a smaller section upon which the throne was mounted. Some illustrations show two, some three sections vertically. The lowest section, the bed of the wagon, was heavily carved and it is this work that appears to be that of English carriage makers rather than of American ship carvers. Its mass and intricacy was never equaled in American work, probably because of the cost. Often titled "The Car of Neptune," this wagon has given rise much speculation concerning its history. At the present state of information it seems that the throne was removed and a great statue of Neptune driving sea horses substituted, possibly in 1880. It burned in a fire in winter quarters in 1887.

The rest of the parade consisted of the two elephants, one of them named Gipsy (sic), and an array of mounted people. While it was a good one, the Barnum parade was no larger, at least on paper, than those of Adam Forepaugh or the VanAmburgh Menagerie. The majority of shows, however, were content to confine their parading to the passage of their bandwagon.

J. J. Justice was the manager of the advance and his minions distributed such verbiage as "the largest and most attractive exhibitions on earth" and "one hundred thousand curiosities."

Perhaps the most interesting notice they distributed was the one that read:

> This Great Moral Exhibition is visited by eminent divines and by the best and most refined members of Society everywhere. No person need visit the Equestrian Performance unless they choose to do so.

Moral opposition to circuses still existed in rural and small town America in enough force to call for such messages. However, a visit to the museum and menagerie were considered educational and for those who did not want to see women in tights or hear the blasphemy of clowns there was still reason to purchase a ticket.

The arena performance, at this distance, does not appear to have been superior to that offered by competitors of Barnum, yet it was by no means inferior either. It began with one of the early spectacles, *Sprites of the Silvery Shower*, an entree piece on horseback. The rest of the program included equestriennes Mlle. Pauline Hindley, advertised as being "*L'artiste première du Cirque Français*" (who died during the season from injuries received in a fall from her horse in Rome, NY); Mlle. Carlotta DaVinci, "the premiere sprite of the elfin drama, *Pluie d'argent*"; Maria Celeste Girardeau, "dashing and brilliant" bareback rider; the Marion Sisters, hurdle riders (in their American debut); and Mrs. Dan Castello. What was described as first-class English, French, German, and Italian artists, tumbers, leapers, gymnasts, acrobats, and riders, "secured by special engagement expressly for P. T. Barnum's Great Hippodrome," included such unidentifiables as Smith, English, Cook, Hartnette, Giovani, Fitzgerald, and Heimberger. There were also the adolescent prodigies of bareback riding, Harry and Johnny Castello.

A few performers had names familiar to American audiences. William Dutton, the star bareback rider, was well traveled and well respected. David R. Hawley and Thomas E. Miaco were a recognized flying gymnastic team. Then there was the versatile Burnell Runnells and sons, Bonnie and Freddie, gymnasts and riders. Professor Charles White was in charge of the wild beast department. And Dan Castello performed his school of highly trained equines, the featured being the trick horse, Czar, "as black as a raven's wing," and the comic mules, Artemus and Timothy.

From Brooklyn the route led to New Jersey, Connecticut, Massachusetts, New Hampshire, Maine and New York State. At Waterville, Maine they turned back because the small towns weren't able to support such a large show. It must have been here that Coup began wondering how to avoid small towns. They went west to Buffalo along the Erie Canal and returned to the Hudson by the Elmira–Binghampton path so many shows have trod. They closed in Harlem on October 28 and then opened in the American Institute Building on November 12 for a winter show that closed January 6.

Attendance was high, as we said, and some examples are 15,000 at three shows in Portland, Maine; 8,000 at one show in Albany; 9,000 at one performance in Rochester, New York. The Auburn, New York newspaper said that 20,000 people came to town on show day. The city fathers of Waterville, Maine, somehow guessed there'd be a crowd and erected a tent for those who came from such a distance that they had to sleep in town.

On April 23 in Morristown, New Jersey, the show purchased four black Spanish mules which they hitched to the cookhouse wagon; Theodore Conklin of Delavan, the teamster. The next day the wagon, bringing up the rear of the column, was struck at a grade crossing in Cranford. Bystanders, some of whom yelled to Conklin that the train was coming, said that the mules became unmanageable at the sound of the train and could not be turned from the tracks. The train struck the wheel team and demolished the wagon, the lead team being unhurt. Conklin was killed as was the cook, a black man named Edward Dyer. Tommy Welsh, an employee riding on the wagon, was so badly injured he died in a few days.

At a coroner's inquest held immediately after the accident it was determined that Conklin was thrown fifty feet through the air to land on his head. He died of a broken neck. The engineer was bruised by flying debris and there was blood—from the mules—all along the smoking car, which in those days was just behind the tender.

The injured were placed on another train, at Barnum's orders, and taken to Bellevue Hospital in New York. It was there that Walsh died. The coroner's jury found no liability could be imputed to the railroad, the Central of New Jersey.[16]

In contrast to today's folk belief that "the show must go on," is the editorial comment in the Elizabeth newspaper that "the heartlessness of circus men was shown on Thursday in this town. After three of

P. T. BARNUM'S
Museum, Menagerie, Caravan & Hippodrome.

Norwalk 25 April 1871.

Mr. *Sammu Dunham*

Rev. Sir.

In asking your acceptance of this Complimentary Ticket, which will admit you and your Lady, it is with the distinct assurance that my chief object in presenting this Great Exhibition to the public is to benefit them, as well as to instruct and amuse; that nothing either in look, word, or gesture will be permitted in any of my Entertainments at all incompatible with that honor and respectability which have always characterized my former amusement enterprises, or in any manner derogatory to the dignity or conscientious scruples of a Christian Minister, his wife and family.

My Manager and assistants are men of families, temperate and abstemious in their habits, and endeavor to employ only such persons as uphold teetotalism, decorum, and good morals.

Your Obedient Servant,

P. T. Barnum

Exhibits *Friday May 5*

The Day Exhibitions are usually less crowded than those of the Evening.

their number had been killed and others seriously wounded by the railroad accident, they went through their buffoon exhibitions the same afternoon and evening as though nothing had occurred."

Also, in Elizabeth, on the 27th of April, despite the warnings of a flagman, a herd of ponies and mules from the circus crossed the tracks as a train was approaching. The engineer was able to stop before striking them. The disregard of danger at railroad crossings in those days is obvious to anyone reading the newspapers of the time. In city after city grade crossings had to be abolished because of the numerous accidents.

In Boston the *Transcript* was taken with Barnum's parade. The review reads:[17]

> [The parade] culminated in the most magnificent chariot which ever passed through our streets ... a remarkable production composed of gilt and glass. Its height is no less surprising than its brilliancy and at its greatest altitude a lady was seated viewing with unconcern the doings of the world below. The second and less pretensious chariot was drawn by eight horses and several camels which, as they passed, the *Transcript* office, scented the contents of the Frog Pond and left for that oasis without reference to the continuity of the procession. They went with a considerable vengeance for a short time, but were brought back into the traces.

The circus was in Boston a week, from the 12th to the 17th of June. They continued north and by July 19 were in Manchester, New Hampshire. The *Daily Union* took the troupe to task, saying that the circus was very badly managed. There were not enough seats so the ring performance could be seen by only half the people present and, in addition, it was very dusty in the tent. The menagerie was pronounced excellent and the wax figures supremely ridiculous, but the parade was said to be very long and splendid. Twelve thousand spectators attended the three shows there.[18]

The Portsmouth *Journal*, in advance of the July 21 date, printed the comments of the Reverend G. H. Emerson which had appeared in the New York *Christian Leader* and they were:

> ... the success which everywhere attends Barnum's great show ought to be evidence to the managers who furnish amusement to the public that profanity and indecency of speech and gesture—all of which Mr. Barnum excludes by promptly and indignantly discharging the offender—are not of the nature of supply meeting a popular demand.

However, despite the minister's statement, the giant, Monsieur Goliath, got into an imbroglio with one Waldron, a milkman in Dover, New Hampshire, on July 22 and was fined twenty dollars by the local magistrate. This man was advertised as being over eight feet tall and must have been quit an adversary for the milkman.[19]

They went to Portland, Maine where the editor of the *Daily Press* said that the street show was more like the traditional caravan displays of a quarter century ago than any he had seen for a long time. He must have been referring to the menagerie parades of the fifties in which long lines of cages were a feature. The first tent (the museum) reminded him of the old American Museum with it curiosities, statuary, wax and mechanical figures. This, of course, was just what Barnum intended. Interestingly, the editor complained that the tickets had been announced as going on sale at 9:00 a.m., but that forty minutes was consumed in the selling of Barnum's autobiography before the ticket wagon opened.[20]

There was another accident involving a train in Augusta, Maine as the caravan left on the morning of July 29 for their stand in Waterville. At 3:30 a.m. a team descending Winthrop Hill took fright at a train which was crossing the road and dashed toward it. The teamster managed to turn them aside before they struck the cars, but the wagon overturned. A Mr. Summerfield, a member of the staff, riding in the wagon received a broken arm and the giant, Monsieur Goliath, was so bruised that he missed several days of work.[21]

In Waterville, the town we reported as providing tents for the rural show-goers, many arrived from as far away as seventy-five miles (the circus billed a radius of fifty to seventy-five miles). All morning on the 29th crowds poured in by carriage, wagon, ox cart, and afoot. The sale of liquor was banned for the day and the city put out barrels of ice-water for public use. Just as the morning performance was ending, two full excursion trains arrived, one of twenty-seven cars from Bangor (where the circus had decided not to show) and another of seventeen cars from Belfast. It was announced that a continuous performance would be given so that all could be accommodated and the tear-down came at 9:00 p.m.[22]

It was at this point that the route was changed and the caravan headed west into New Hampshire, playing Lewiston, Maine, on the way. Here the first and only reported "clem" of the season took place. According to local reports it began when one of the circus employees for no apparent reason knocked an elderly man to the ground and taking out a knife, threatened to cause him more harm. The man's sons took him away and rounded up a few friends who proceeded to shower rocks at the departing show. They claimed to have staved in the side of one wagon and badly used the grand chariot in the course of the night, in the words of the newspaper.[23]

In Albany, which they played on August 22, Barnum's crew saw their first "day and date." Dan Rice's Paris Pavilion Circus played a four day engagement, from the 21st through the 24th. The Albany *Argus* reporter was quite taken with Rice's pavilion—this was the wooden, collapsible structure he was hauling about the country that year. If we are to believe that gentleman, Rice carried the day though Barnum attracted 8,000 souls despite wet weather, muddy grounds, and a lot outside the city.[24]

For the rest of the season, a swing through New York State, little is found in newspaper reports beyond the usual compliments. It was one of the most successful seasons a circus had had in America to that time. It cannot be doubted that it was Barnum's name that brought the crowds those miles into town on circus day, but once there, what a magnificent thing they saw. The tents and horses and wagons and people were in profusion such as no circus had theretofore displayed. The parade was as fine a one as any offered, the museum and menagerie departments were perhaps the best that could be viewed in that year. The only weakness in the whole presentation was the lack of crowd control in the arena. It must have been serious because so many comments were made about it.

A Connecticut newspaper editor, James M. Bailey, of the Danbury *News* wrote a humorous piece about his experiences in visiting the Barnum show in 1871 and part of it read:[25]

> When I got inside the large tent I was surprised. A sea of faces spread out before me. The tier seats were crowded, the ring seats were crowded, gangways were crowded. It was a mass of suffocation, fun and sweat. I really enjoyed the sight. Here, embraced in an area of a few hundred yards, might be observed—
>
> "Why don't that bald-headed reptile set down?" cried a coarse voice behind me. I looked around. A red-faced illiterate man was glowering down upon me from a tier seat. I cast a sorrowful glance upon him and sat down. There were fifty or sixty people between me and the ring. I had not made any calculation for this when I came, and so I didn't appreciate it. Occasionally somebody hollered, "Down in front." I had an

excellent view of the tent. I knew there was something going on in the ring, but if I had been prostrated on my dying couch I could not have told what it was. But I knew whenever a different act commenced, because he people in front of me stood up on the seats, and the folks behind me put their children on my head, and their umbrellas down my back, and remarked audibly to each other, "Was there ever anything like it?" And I, staring idiotically into the back of the man in front of me, fervently hoped there was not. But all things have an end, and the dreary afternoon performance was not an exception. The last act was performed, the clown finally convulsed the audience, the children in the rear were pulled out of my hair, and I was permitted to fall over, roll around, and eventually get on my feet. With the crowd gone, I stole back to the tent and took one fond piercing glance at what I had not yet seen—the ring.

The solution to this—the introduction of the two-ring arena—in 1872 was the way in which that season improved upon 1871. Whether the adoption of railway travel in the same year was an improvement for the public remains to be seen. Of the principals, certainly Coup and Castello were pleased with the season and Barnum—at least in his autobiography—was elated. Not only had he made a lot of money, but his name had been spread again over the whole northeast, and one can almost say with certainty that that was, to him, the greatest reward.

NOTES

[1] Yadon, "RBBB Actual Formation," p. 8.
[2] Syracuse *Standard* (n.d., n.p.n.).
[3] Saxon, *P. T Barnum*, p. 231.
[4] New York *Clipper*, May 16, 1891.
[5] Interview of P. T. Barnum, clipping, *The Era,* July 29, 1877 (n.p.n.).
[6] Barnum, *Struggles and Triumphs*, p. 852.
[7] Syracuse *Standard, op. cit.*
[8] *P. T. Barnum Annual Courier*, 1871.
[9] J. Fred Crosby, "The Early Days of Barnum's 'Greatest on Earth,'" p. 49.
[10] The New York *Clipper* gave the number ninety-five, the New York *Times* one hundred.
[11] New York *Clipper*, October 21, 1871.
[12] Stuart Thayer, "Joseph E. Warner: Pioneer of the Three Tent Circus", p. 20.
[13] The Portsmouth *Journal* reports five, the Boston *Journal*, eight.
[14] Boston *Journal* quoted in *Struggles and Triumphs,* 1872 edition, p. 859.
[15] New York *Clipper*, November 25, 1871. Barnum claims he paid $15,000 for the Great Golden Chariot in England.

[16] New Jersey *Journal* (Elizabeth), May 2, 1871.
[17] Quoted in Exeter, New Hampshire *News-Letter*, July 14, 1871.
[18] Manchester *Daily Union,* July 20, 1871.
[19] Dover *Inquirer,* July 27, 1871.
[20] Portland *Daily Press*, July 26, 1871.
[21] P. T. Barnum, *Struggles and Triumphs,* 1872 edition, p. 860..
[22] *Ibid.*
[23] Lewiston *Weekly Journal*, August 3, 1871.
[24] Albany *Argus*, August 23, 1871.
[25] James M. Bailey, *Life in Danbury,* p. 60.

III
P. T. BARNUM'S GREAT TRAVELING EXPOSITION AND WORLD'S FAIR, 1872

At the close of the 1871 summer season, the Barnum circus went into the Empire Rink Building at Third Avenue and 63rd Street in New York for a winter's run. This was on November 13; the stand ended on January 6. At that time, according to the Chindahl files, Barnum was willing to move the circus to Racine, Wisconsin, if sufficient land could be purchased for a winter quarters. Dan Castello was a resident of Racine and presumably suggested such an arrangement. He located twelve acres west of the Chicago & Northwestern tracks at Doud Street, which were available for $12,000. However, he apparently reckoned without Mrs. Castello, who liked her home and didn't want to move. Someone else then purchased the Doud Street property. Later, Castello found another parcel near 12th and Main Streets, but his wife still refused to move. Why it was necessary that Castello live at the quarters is not answered in the reference. Perhaps his plan was to purchase the land and lease it to the show and he needed to sell his house in order to accomplish this. By that much did Racine, Wisconsin, miss becoming possibly the circus center that Bridgeport eventually became. Barnum's interest in Bridgeport and its proximity to New York would likely have led to the situation we know, however, Mrs. Castello or no.

Eighteen-seventy-two was, of course, the year in which the Barnum circus went on rails. If one reads Barnum's autobiography, this innovation was his idea; if one reads Coup's *Sawdust and Spangles,* it was Coup's idea. Regardless, it was Coup's task to accomplish the change, and both men agree that it was done in order to avoid playing in small towns in which attendance was limited. The wagon show could only move as fast as the horses could pull it, fifteen to twenty miles a day on average. Having to show every day meant stopping at the nearest town in many of which the potential audience would not pay the overhead of the day's traveling. But using the railroad, "we could ignore the small places," Coup wrote, "and travel only from one big town to another, thereby drawing the cream of the trade from the adjacent small towns instead of trying to give an exhibition in each."[1]

They were not the first to think of this, as Coup acknowledges. In 1851, Gilbert R. Spalding financed "The Railroad Circus," a show that traveled up and down what became the New York Central Railroad. In 1856, Spalding had one of his own circuses mounted on nine custom-built railroad cars, but abandoned the effort after one season. From 1866 to 1873, Lewis B. Lent's New York Circus traveled on chartered trains, the first successful adoption to railroads.

Coup claimed that he was turned down by several railroads when he broached the idea to them, but eventually he won over the Pennsylvania and with that began arranging car leases.

The details of the railroad equipment and its use have been well covered by others, so we will not explicate them here.[2] However, it is important that the number of cars has been found to be sixty-five, divided into two trains.[3] Researchers have always been fascinated, and rightly so, by the 1872 Barnum train; oddly, that interest did not exist at the time as almost nothing has been found to illustrate either the loading or unloading activities. This leads us to conclude that the operation was used by other shippers and therefore had become mundane.

The main advantage of the new system was the avoidance of small towns, as we said, and in 1872 only six towns of less than 3,000 population were played (ignoring nine places the population of which is unknown to us) out of 145 stands. Because the show had to go where the tracks went, and they wanted to perform every day, they very occasionally were forced to play a small town on their way to more populous areas. This happened, at the most, once in ten days.

In addition to the expense of leasing the railroad cars and paying the way bills, Coup had to add a train crew to the payroll. This consisted of a master of transportation, his assistant, and twenty-nine workmen.

This number assuredly made a small dent in the gross, which increased two-and-a-half times over that of 1871. An Ohio newspaper commented: "It has cost as much money to fit out [Barnum's] great traveling show as the British government paid for its famous expedition in search of John Franklin."[4]

Barnum was advertised as the proprietor and Coup as the manager. Barnum had a 40% interest in the firm; Coup, Castello and Samuel H. Hurd, Barnum's son in law and show treasurer, had 20% each.

Barnum had capitalized the 1871 show and held 2/3 of the ownership. He also had a 3% override, *i.e.*, he received that percentage of the gross over and above any dividends paid. Whether that arrangement continued in 1872 is not known.

Edward Buckley, one of the many Delavan residents with the circus, had been Coup's assistant in 1871. He was replaced by fellow-townsman Luke Tilden for 1872. Buckley and his brother moved over to the more profitable privilege side of the concern, having the 1872 concert.

Tilden, rising from 1871 parade manager to be Coup's assistant, certainly improved his position. Others who moved up were S. H. Hurd from assistant treasurer to treasurer and W. C. Crum from director of publications to general agent.

Hold-overs in the same capacities as 1871 included Dr. A. C. Berry, veterinarian; Joseph Baker, boss canvasman (called "master of pavillions"); Charles White, lion trainer and menagerie superintendent; and George Coup, W. C.'s brother, at the candy privilege.

Charles C. Pell, longtime agent (we first find him in 1847), was the trainmaster; J. L. Hutchinson, future Barnum partner, was a press agent; Ben Lusbie, general ticket agent; Fritz Hartman, band leader; Stump Robinson, ring stock boss. Another recognizable name was Page Buckley, Mathew's son, who worked in the cookhouse for his brothers, Harry and Ed.

It was in 1872 that the phrase "Greatest Show on Earth," was first used by Barnum. It may have been true; comparisons are difficult. No other proprietor offered a museum as large as his; the menagerie might have been surpassed by Forepaugh's twenty-eight cages; James E. Cooper's ring presentation was at least as strong. As for street parades, no showmen could come near the panoply offered by Howes' Great London.

In management, however, we think Coup had the edge on everyone. He took this new method, railroading, and a large show and traveled up to one hundred miles a night and, he claimed, " ... visited all the cities and important towns from New York to Bangor, Maine, then west as far as Omaha and north as far as St. Paul ... without missing a connection or losing a show."

This was an amazing effort and one that managers have used as an example ever since. However, they did not play Bangor, as Coup stated, or anyplace else in New England. Nor did they go to Omaha,

P. T. BARNUM'S GREAT Traveling World's Fair!

Consisting of Museum, Menagerie, Caravan, Hippodrome, Polytechnic Institute, International Zoological Garden, and Dan. Castello's Chaste and Refined Circus,

In Six Separate Collossal Tents

Everything will be Exhibited as Advertised.

Will Exhibit in Fond du Lac Friday, September 27, 1872,

Giving three full and undivided exhibitions each day of the entire seven shows, morning, afternoon and evening.

Doors open at 10 A. M., 1 and 7 P. M. Hippodrome performances commence at 11 A. M., and 2 and 8 P.M.

Admission to the Seven Collossal Shows, only 50 cents; children half price.

This is positively the Largest and most Attractive combination of exhibitions ever known and remains absolutely without a parallel in the history of the world. It embraces in the various departments of the exposition

One hundred thousand Living and Representative Curiosities!

One thousand Men and Horses!

Five hundred rare living wild Animals, Birds, Reptiles and Marine Monsters.

One hundred of the best performers in the world!

Ten tents cover five acres; 3 trains of 38 cars each; 2 locomotives to each train!

Seven Superior Exhibitions in six separate Collossal tents!

Ten times more than ever seen in any ordinary show.

More than a Million Capital invested!

Daily expenses exceed Five Thousand Dollars!

The entire pavillions are brilliantly illuminated in the evening by 1,000 gas jets!

Excursion trains will run on all the railroads for a distance of 75 miles to convey passengers to P. T Barnum's great show at half fare.

Free admission to all who purchase the Life of P. T. Barnum, written by himself, nearly 900 pages, muslin gilt, steel portrait, 32 full page engravings, reduced from $3.50 to $1.50, and a 50 cent ticket given to each purchaser. To be had of the agent on the day of exhibition.

Nothing like it ever seen on earth.

Topeka, Kansas, being their western-most stop. The last stand was in Detroit on October 29 and 30. From there they returned to New York, a trip requiring ten days.

Six separate tents for one price of admission, the ads read. However, there were complaints along the way of people having to pay another fifteen cents to see the Bunnell brothers' sideshow.

This indicates some confusion concerning the number of tents. The show had ten tents on the lot, four of them presumably for horses and equipment. The five that could be seen for fifty cents were:

1—Automatons. Wax figures that played instruments, breathed and made head motions. Birds that flew. Ships that sailed. Cars which ran. Ancient armor. A family of Fiji cannibals. A Digger Indian from the Yosemite Valley of California.

2—Menagerie. Contained twenty of the small cross-cages of the day. The unusual specimens were a rhinoceros, a giraffe, two sea lions, and a supposed gorilla, which was most likely a chimpanzee.

3—Led Animals. A tent-full of camels, dromedaries, and two elephants.

4—Strange People. Admiral Dot, the midget. The Albino family. The bearded child. Anna E. Leake, the girl without arms.

5—The arena.

Three shows a day, at eleven, two, and eight o'clock was the usual order and the only time they seem to have deviated from that schedule was in Kansas City on August 14 when a railroad wreck ahead of the circus train delayed them long enough to allow only two performances.

What the public saw in the ring "surpasses anything seen in this city before," said the paper in LaCrosse, Wisconsin.[5] Admission was fifty cents and one ticket passed a person through the whole show. Purchasers of Barnum's autobiography, usually costing $3.50, paid $1.50 and received a ticket as well.

The people came in droves. The one consistent observation in the newspapers was of the constant press of persons arriving to view the parade and the big show.

"Before five o'clock this morning the roll of wheels upon the streets sounded forth the potency of advertising. Within an hour the incoming carriages had increased in number until the main streets ... were crowded as with a procession. Thousands have come by the railroad alone," said the Akron *Daily Beacon* of 15 June.

"The largest crowd ever in Decatur is here today ... while the sun was rising parties were running to and fro to secure safe quarters for their teams," said the Decatur, Illinois, *Daily Republican* of 30 August.

"There has been no such crowd known before in Kansas City. The old exposition ground was literally packed with humanity," said the Wyandotte, Kansas, *Kansas Gazette* of August 15.

"We were all through the war, and used to think that there was no equal to a lot of hungry soldiers at the dinner hour. But the rush inside the great museum for the circus entrance beats anything we ever saw, and the great human wave kept swelling on with no let up," said the Delavan, Wisconsin, *Republican* of October 3.

The most profound change in the arena itself was the adoption of the two ring configuration. Dan Castello claimed the credit for this improvement:[6]

> Barnum came to me and asked what we were going to do, as the canvas was getting so big that the people could not see. I told him that we would have to put in two rings. Then we did it in the proper way, too. We had two companies as near alike as possible, and had the performance of one ring duplicated in the other. So, in reality we had two circuses in one. That was better for the circus and better for the people, as the performers would do better work. I sat near the two rings and controlled everything, the music, the performers, and the ring men, by a bell.

W. C. Coup, in his autobiography, said, "Our experience with the vast crowds of the season before had given us the idea of building two rings, and giving a double performance."[7] Barnum did not comment on the change, so Castello may truly have originated it. Incidentally, his use of a bell to perform as equestrian director was still in practice as late as 1903.

In the arena the crowds saw Dan Castello's highly-trained horses, Czar, Senator and Flying Cloud; the horse-riding goat Alexis; Charles White in the lion cage; James Melville and his family on horseback; Lazelle and Milson on the flying trapeze; and Gipsy, the performing elephant. They also saw clowns, acrobats, leapers, all the stuff of the nineteenth century circus, none of it new, most of it the same as was seen on the Barnum lot in 1871.

James Melville was one of the leading bareback riders of his day. His rivals were Charles Fish of the Lent show, James Robinson on

WILD FIJI CANNIBALS!
Captives of war, lately ransomed from King Thokambau by Mr. Barnum, at a cost of $15,000.

his own circus, and Bob Stickney of the John Robinson company. Choosing among them would be very difficult.

Melville's son Frank was a pad rider, son George was a bareback rider, and little Alexander rode a pony act. Lazelle and Milson performed on a single trapeze and dismounted by flying from it to a hanging rope which they slid down. Monte Verde was a contortionist, Wash Antonio an acrobat, Gus Lee and George Madden the clowns. Excepting Melville, none of the company was head and shoulders over the competition. The show didn't advertise their skills as individuals. The Akron, Ohio, *Daily Beacon* commented that John Robinson's Circus, which had proceeded Barnum in that city, was actually superior.[8]

The big thing about Barnum's circus was Barnum. If it was Barnum's show, it was worth seeing and the massive advertising effort summoned the crowds from miles around. The Cleveland, Ohio, *Plain Dealer* of 18 June editorialized that the reason for Barnum's success "it will be noted, is that Mr. Barnum advertises. He has on exhibition and

Revolving Temple of Juno, advertised in the 1872 Advance Courier as being drawn by a team of twenty Bactrian camels, Asiatic and African elephants, and Arabian dromedaries, while upon elevated seats, beneath a rich Oriental canopy, was displayed a beautiful *tableau vivant* representing various gods and goddesses surrounding the mythological queen, all in all, forming a unique and imposing picture.

Parade and Museum Wagons

keeps impressing on everybody's mind that he is coming with a big show."

Part of the advertising, of course, was the daily street parade. In 1872 it was not far different from that of 1871, which is to say that it compared well with its rivals, excepting only the one presented by Howes' Great London.

Two agents in a buggy led the procession, followed by an elegant wagon devoted to the sale of Barnum's autobiography. Then came the "Orpheus" bandwagon pulled by twelve camels and four horses. Both this and the "Juno" we described in our previous chapter. Next came twenty cages, each with a four-horse hitch. Some of these had automata on top, as they had the year before. Next came several ponies ridden by boys after which appeared a miniature coach pulled by four ponies and containing Admiral Dot, the midget. The large, revolving "Temple of Juno" with a ten-camel hitch then approached, after which were twenty mounted men wearing suits of armor. There was another band, apparently hired locally at each stand, and finally more cages and the two elephants. Somewhere in the line was a glass-enclosed snake den complete with a snake charmer festooned with reptiles. This was the first glass sided cage to appear on American streets. Museum cages as well as animal dens were common in street shows of the day, so it is not possible to know the exact number of each, as they looked alike on the exterior.

Coup tried to operate a "Sunday school" show as they came to be known. We find no references to any disreputable actions on the part of circus employees, but such a crowd puller attracted every thief and pickpocket who could afford train fare. The Akron paper printed a list of house break-ins and picked pockets on circus day. The show detectives apparently refused to eject the thieves they knew of, claiming they were there to protect Barnum's people, not the public.[9] Other than this type of depredation, the show moved across the country almost without incident. This was an amazing feat when one considers that sixty-some railroad cars were unloaded each morning, loaded each night, and a vast vacant lot (two acres at a minimum) was transformed into a thriving canvas city in between. Three cages were demolished in a switching accident between Erie and Corry, Pennsylvania; both engines and several cars were derailed in Cleveland; a member of the train crew drowned while bathing in a creek in Canton, Ohio; a teamster did the same while watering horses in Hamilton, Ohio. "My men got rest, were fresh, and ready for work," Coup said of the advantages of rail movement and the lack of accidents reinforces that statement.

There were no clems reported in the press. We would guess that 130 working men would suffice to disabuse any local toughs from the idea of "raising dust," as the contemporary idiom had it.

An ordinance lay before the Cleveland city council which would have forbid circuses and menageries from appearing in that city. Barnum arrived the same day the ordinance was proposed, June 17. The *Plain Dealer* cautioned: " ... thirty thousand people, mostly from the poorer classes, may be attracted to an exhibition of this nature in a single day, we should think that a body who are supposed to represent the people would think twice before depriving them of the privilege."[10]

There were three ticket wagons on the lot, one of which was reserved for ladies. Twenty-eight thousand admissions were sold in Cleveland in two days. In Sandusky, Ohio (population 13,000), there were 26,000 sales for three performances. In Harrisburg, Pennsylvania, 30,000 people attended on May 13; the receipts were announced as being $8,000. We think this figure is the day's profit, as 30,000 tickets would produce something close to $15,000. in receipts.

So much money was being shipped east by express from the circus—shipped under W. C. Coup's name—that the express company suspected it was the profits of a gambling operation and had detectives investigate.

Eighteen-seventy-two was not a good year for the circus business. Hot weather, especially in the west, had a tendency to keep the crowds down. It was an election year, always a slow time in the entertainment business since it focuses the people's attention away from frivolity. There was a late spring, thus the wagon shows were delayed in getting started because of bad roads. Twenty-two percent (10 of 45) of the 1872 circuses closed early. The Barnum show, however, grossed a million dollars, the first circus to achieve such a season s take. The profits exceeded $200,000.[11]

The expenses were tremendous, of course. Over and above the cost of framing the show was the daily $600 to $1,000 for rail transportation. It cost $3,000 to $4,000 a day to keep the enterprise going. Coup didn't skimp in hiring or spending. He said years later: "Barnum had a propensity not to pinch pennies. Such expenditures, if applied to commercial (as opposed to entertainment) undertakings, would prove eminently disastrous."[12]

Speed and order, these were the by-words by which the show was operated. As is now well-known, in labor-intensive work efficiency is increased by increasing the number of workers. As we noted, Coup's force, exclusive of menagerie men, numbered 130.

"Each man knows his duty and when a day's show is ended the vast tent and immense properties of all kinds are in two or three hours transported to the cars and are rolling away fifty to a hundred miles to be spread in another city."[13] That was the comment of a New Hampshire editor. Modern observers, aware of the efficiency and discipline required to put up and tear down a big railroad circus, may not wonder at Coup's ability to organize the 1872 operation, but it must be remembered that he had no experience of it prior to 1872.

Drunkenness among the employees was strictly forbidden; any man so observed was discharged immediately, according to press reports, a not inconsiderable attitude in the nineteenth century. "There is none of the rowdyism among the employees that is so common to traveling shows" said the Dayton *Journal*. The men were fed on the lot since the vast army could not be expected to find board and room in hotels. A check-room on wheels was provided so that their personal goods could be protected.

Newspaper commentators, our most abundant source of information on shows of that era, were impressed by the orderliness, as we noted. The amount of advertising and the efforts of the press agents were also subjects of interest. J. L. Hutchinson and D. S. Thomas made it habit to show newsmen about the show each day and to answer their questions. So much of this foretells the modern practice that one

wonders if Coup might not qualify for the title of father of large circus operation.

Kit Clarke, a writer for the New York *Clipper* and erstwhile circus press agent said of Coup after the 1871 show was in the barn: "There are very few men who could have managed the Barnum show as Billy Coup has done, for, besides displaying great executive ability and a wonderful foresight, he is always the gentleman, whether dealing with a governor or a canvasman; and hereafter, when the great Barnum show is mentioned, much of its success will be attributed to its able manager."[14]

The rhetoric of newspaper ad copy is seldom accepted as reality, yet we think a fitting close to this narrative can be taken from Barnum's 1872 press efforts, viz: "Of the millions of people who have visited Barnum's World's Fair since it left New York (transported by three trains of forty cars each), there is not a man, woman or child who will not say that it is not only twenty times the largest, but it is also the only legitimate, undivided, unepitomized, most expensive and elaborate of exhibitions ever known...."

NOTES

[1] W. C. Coup, *Sawdust and Spangles*, p. 61.
[2] See Fred Dahlinger, Jr., "The Development of the Railroad Circus."
[3] Robert J. Loeffler's analysis of newspaper reports to determine the actual number of cars in Barnum's 1872 train, pp. 35-43
[4] Toledo *Blade*, June 27, 1872.
[5] LaCrosse (WI) *Republican and Leader*, September 28, 1872.
[6] Clipping, Syracuse *Standard*, 1899.
[7] Coup, *op. cit.*, p. 63.
[8] Akron, (OH) *Daily Beacon*, June 17, 1872.
[9] *Ibid.*
[10] Cleveland (OH) *Plain Dealer*, June 18, 1872.
[11] C. C. Sturtevant article, a clipping in the Chindahl papers.
[12] New York *Clipper*, May 16, 1891.
[13] Portsmouth (NH) *Daily Evening Times*, May 28, 1872.
[14] New York *Clipper*, November 25, 1871.

IV
P. T. BARNUM'S GREAT MUSEUM, MENAGERIE, HIPPODROME AND TRAVELLING WORLD'S FAIR, 1873

The Barnum circus came off the road at the end of the 1872 season, and moved into the Hippotheatron Building on 14th Street in New York. The winter performances were scheduled to begin on November 11, but were postponed one week because of an illness among the horses. Coup set about preparations for 1873. In December, Barnum went to New Orleans to reclaim property he had leased to Pardon A. Older for a circus bearing Barnum's name, partly financed by the old showman. This outfit had left Louisville on November 4, and followed a route through Kentucky, Tennessee, Georgia and Louisiana, ending up in New Orleans. The season was not a success, and after an eight-day stand in New Orleans, Older closed the operation. While Barnum was attending to the salvage, he was informed that the Hippotheatron had burned to the ground.

Returning to New York, Barnum found his partners in despair. Coup was ready to forego traveling in 1873, according to Arthur Saxon, and treasurer Hurd was distressed by the loss of the $50,000 revenue that the winter show was expected to contribute.[1] But Barnum, in his autobiography, said that his own attitude was that "only pluck, courage, and a liberal outlay of money," were necessary to get the show on the road.[2]

Barnum referred to the rebuilding of the circus on the front page of the 1873 courier:

> Although the fire of Dec. 24, 1872, totally destroyed my third museum building, and a magnificent collection of rare animals making my losses by fire, within fifteen years, exceed a million of dollars—I have emerged again from the cinders and smoke with an unimpaired constitution, unabated energies, and a more earnest determination than ever to gratify, as I have always so successfully done, the ever-recurring demands of the amusement-seeking public. Fortunately, I had sent to New Orleans, for exhibition during the holidays, duplicates of nearly all the animals destroyed. And, fortunately also, telegraphic wires and oceanic

cables enable us, in these days, to accomplish more in three months than we could formerly have done in as many years.[3]

None of the horses, wagons, nor any rolling stock had been lost. The performers lost all their property, and several benefit performances were arranged at the Academy of Music, just across the street from the ashes of the Hippotheatron. Barnum himself appeared at these events, and some relief was provided for the performers.

The money loss to the partners was $300,000, by Barnum's statement, and there was but $90,000 insurance. The circus had grossed a million dollars in 1872, which left a profit of about $250,000. This, combined with the insurance proceeds, was available to rebuild the third of the property that had been lost. It would seem to have been enough, though Barnum proceeded to spend lavishly.

Having framed the largest circus in the country in 1871, and having mounted it on the railroads in 1872, the Barnum–Coup forces could only enlarge it in 1873 to surpass what they had already accomplished. There were thirty-eight circuses on tour in 1873, and the partners apparently were not of a mind to be second to any of them.

Coup was in charge of rebuilding the "Greatest Show on Earth," as they now called it, and most of the work was done in New York City. The repairing and redecorating of the 150 wagons (including parade vehicles and cages) was assigned to Fielding & Sons of 41st Street, and Sebastian and Saal on 3rd Avenue. Higgins, the well-known tent maker, at 192 West Street, made the tents, of which there were twelve, including a big top that would seat 13,000 people. R. S. Walker of Allen Street was given a contact for $15,000 worth of banners and costumes. At the shops of William Cummins & Son in Bergen, New Jersey, flat cars were built or refurbished. Six sleeping cars were converted from passenger coaches at New Haven. In Cleveland enough stock cars for 300 horses were newly built or repaired at the McNary & Claflen works.

William Wallace, a taxidermist at 616 Broadway, prepared over 500 birds that were displayed in about twenty museum cages. Poles were made at local shipyards. The parade horses were wintered at Coup's farm in Delavan, Wisconsin; ring horses were boarded at New Brunswick, New Jersey, and Newton, Long Island. The menagerie, once it was recalled from P. A. Older's "Barnum Show" in New Orleans, and with new additions, was housed in Commodore Vanderbilt's stables at 30th Street and Ninth Avenue in New York.

Exterior, Hippotheatron, New York

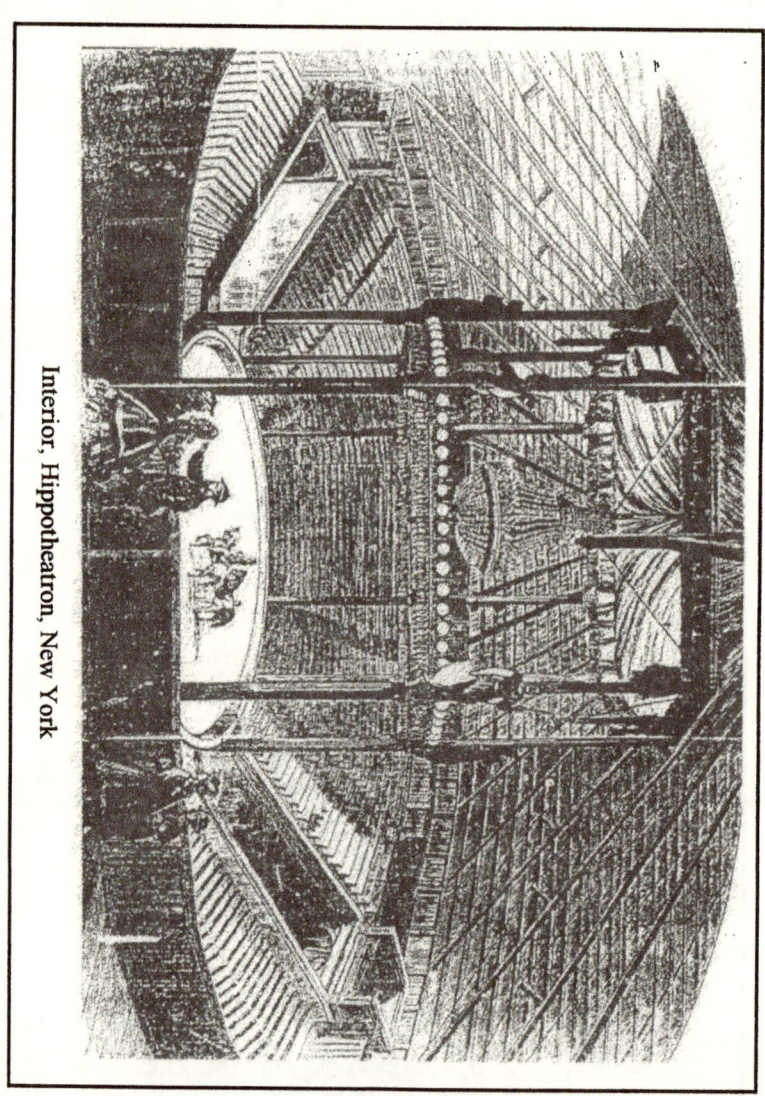

Interior, Hippotheatron, New York

Once all this work was done, and all the animals and performers gathered, the circus opened at the American Institute Building, known as the Rink, at 63rd and Third on Saturday March 29, just ninety-five days after the fire.

As we said, William C. Coup was general manager. Dan Castello was in charge of the circus performance, and S. H. Hurd was the treasurer. These three, each with a twenty percent interest, and Barnum, with forty, made up the show's ownership. Most of the staff, and many of the workmen, were the same as in 1872. Luke Tilden, assistant manager; Ben Lusbie, chief ticket agent; Fritz Hartman, band leader; W. L. Jukes, museum manager; Charles White, menagerie manager; Dr. Asa Berry, veterinarian; Peter Halstead, master of transportation; George Coup, candy privilege; and the Bunnell Brothers, sideshow owners; all occupied the same spots as in the prior season. J. L. Hutchinson, a press agent in 1872, was again in charge of the sale of Barnum's autobiography in 1873, a task which made him a fortune. Charles McLean, superintendent of canvas, came from the Older circus.

The show was much larger than it had been, the 130 workmen of 1872, became 300 in 1873. The canvas crew was the largest section at eighty-eight men. The teamsters numbered forty-five, as did the train crew. Advertising, including the billposters, employed twenty. The menagerie crew had eighteen. Oddly, there were only six ushers to handle crowds up to 13,000.

The first stand after New York, and the first under-canvas stand was Brooklyn on April 16-19. They set up on the Capitoline Grounds, a place where Barnum was to show several times over the next ten seasons.

In the *Courier*, and in daily newspapers advertisements, the statement "20 center pole pavilion" was made. This is confusing to a modern reader, and can only be guessed at as meaning all the center poles on the lot. But even then, the numbers don't make sense. We must conjecture that since one pavilion led to another the total of all the public areas was meant. In fact, the big top had three center poles, and sixty quarter-poles. Coup, in an 1879 interview, said that the tent was 410 by 210 feet with 100 quarter poles. The *Clipper* said it was 300 by 200 feet. C. G. Sturtevant said it was a 150-foot round with three fifty foot middles, which would indicate 300 by 200 feet. There were two rings and a hippodrome track, and on that basis we would expect a 300 by 150 tent with about sixty quarter-poles.

Twenty men traveled a day ahead of the company to prepare the lot (two to three acres) and build the ring banks. Earthen rings were used with wooden stakes atop them from which canvas curtains about two feet high were suspended. As we said, there were two rings, the number first adopted in 1872, as a method of crowd control. They were surrounded by a hippodrome track on which spectacles and races were held. The Barnum show may have been the first to utilize such a layout. The Great Eastern in 1872 claimed the first two-ring circus, but theirs was constructed of two connected center-pole tents.

The performance in this vast canvas show house was one of the largest programs seen to that time. There were sixteen changes, all but three of them involving both rings, plus acts that appeared on the track. Thus, though fifteen or sixteen separate acts had been the industry norm for twenty years, with Barnum this number was doubled in both 1872 and 1873.

Fritz Hartman's orchestra provided an overture, followed by the Grand Hippodrome Entree, a spectacle called *The Halt in the Desert*. This was the fourth straight season that Coup and Castello had begun a program with this theme. Their 1870 circus had used it, and the Barnum shows of 1871, 1872, and 1873 did as well.

The "Human Curiosities" then paraded around the hippodrome track. These people were separate from the Museum Department, as it was known. Nor were they attached to the side show operated by the Bunnell Brothers. Exhibited by S. S. Smith, the group consisted of the midget Admiral Dot; Charles Tripp, the armless boy; "Zip" (William H. Jackson) the "What is it?"; Zaluma Agra, a Circassian lady; and the Fiji Cannibals. The Fiji Islanders were one of the first ethnological exhibits to appear in a circus in America. Barnum & Bailey made much use of such groups. These had appeared first in Barnum's Museum, and were with the circus in 1872.

The rest of the program, by ring number, went in this order:

Ring One	Ring Two
Triple bar act	The Bushnell wire act
Romeo Sebastian, pad riding	Dave Castello, bareback riding
Mathews Family, acrobats	Lazelle & Milson, brother act
Sig. Sebastian, trick horse	Dan Castello, trick horse

Vaulting and tumbling corps
Alexis, the riding goat

Messenger, cannon ball act	D'Atalie, iron jaw
Lucille Watson, principal act	Helen Cooke, principal act
Elephant "Gypsy"	Elephant "Betsey"

Jerry Hopper, stilt act

Dave Castello, scenic act	George North, scenic act
Ladder act	Lazelle & Milson, trapeze
Sig, Sebastian, bareback act	Frank Barry, bareback riding

Comic Scene, "Jockey and Traine"
Concert by the Alabama Slave Minstrels

This is the program that appeared in the route book, published by one Richard A. Arnold, who had also published the 1872 route book. He appears to have left out a number of equestrians, and we would conjecture that what he did was to ignore the acts that appeared on the hippodrome track. As an example, Philo Nathans was listed in the roster as a four-and-six horse rider, but no such act is in the above program. Perhaps Arnold was unable to find a satisfactory method of including these acts, or he might have been limited to a certain number of pages by management.

Clowns still worked in the acts, rather than by themselves. Gus Lee, Walter Aymar, Jerry Hopper, George Mathews and Jerry Mathews were the six Barnum clowns. Frank Whittaker was the equestrian director, Horace Nichols, the ringmaster. "Doc" James Thayer was the head ticket-taker, and these three old timers must have spent many hours in reminiscence of their wagon show days.

The performers worked ten to fifteen minutes (compared to a modern show's limit of about eight). The three-hour show cost 50¢ for adults, 75¢ for reserved seats. Children paid 25¢. A purchaser of Barnum's autobiography at $1.50 (reduced from $3 in 1872) received a free ticket. That the audience got their money's worth seems obvious. Sig. Sebastian, Lucille Watson and Frank Barry were all true stars of the ring. The Mathews Family, eight acrobats, were newly arrived from England, where their work had been well received. The D'Atalies were a top strength act from France. The Bushnells, man and wife, were almost always mentioned in reviews. They juggled, but also presented an impalement act in which Mrs. Bushnell let her husband throw knives and axes at her.

The Castellos, the Bushnells, George North, and Lazelle & Millson were repeating their 1872 appearances on the program. James Melville, the leading rider in the previous season, was gone, and

Barnum Dressing Room, from Sketches by Joseph Becker
[*Frank Leslie's Illustrated Newspaper*, July 12, 1873]

his absence was the greatest difference between this season and 1872. Comparisons of the programs of the leading (in size) circuses of that season do not reveal an overwhelming difference in the talent presented. Barnum, of course, had the edge in numbers.

Where the Barnum effort had a decided advantage was in his museum, which was a miniature version of his former permanent exhibition in New York. Under the direction of W. L. Jukes, the great constructor of automata, this department mirrored the intense nineteenth-century public interest in machinery carried to rather absurd heights. There was Professor Faber's talking machine (a woman's disembodied head which seemed to speak); "busy city" tableaus of Jupiter's palace, a Louis XVI hunting scene, the siege of Paris, the games of Olympus and the like. A portrait gallery of American presidents, and internationally famous men (not a single woman) was featured. A large group of "Roger's Figures," as they're now called, was included. There were automaton bell ringers, a grotto of Calypso, the garden of the Hesperides, five hundred stuffed birds, some of which sang. All this was probably worth the 50¢ show ticket, not to mention the menagerie and the hippodrome.

The "Living Curiosities" we mentioned as appearing on the track at the beginning of the performance. They also occupied a separate tent (not to be confused with the Bunnell Brothers' side show), and this arrangement seems odd to us, for why should they be in two parts of the show? In addition to those we named above, there were Modoc and Digger Indians from California, and a seven year-old bearded girl.

In the Bunnel side-show, a separate operation, were Colonel Routh Goshen, the "Arabian" giant, who was actually an African-American from Middlebush, New Jersey, seven feet, eleven inches tall, and 620 pounds in weight; Isaac Sprague, a living skeleton; Mme. Clark, a fat lady; two albino ladies, Ella Mann and Etta Rogers; and Maximo and Bartola, the famous Aztec children. It cost 15¢ to see this group.

The menagerie was as extensive as any, and lacked only a hippopotamus of the greater prizes. Barnum had lost four giraffes in the Hippotheatron fire, and secured two replacements, one of which was kept in reserve in Bridgeport against further loss. The rhinoceros had survived because he was with the Older circus at the time of the fire. This animal had been imported in 1871, and would survive to the end of the 1873 road season. There were four elephants, two of which, Gypsy and Betsey, performed. The caged animals occupied nearly thirty wagons. The show advertised fifty, but about twenty of these were museum wagons, mainly stuffed birds. There were live birds, as well, from cassowaries to humming birds. There were the usual lions, tigers, leopards, cheetahs, a polar bear, wart hog, tapir, sea lions, all the "world in tribute," as the *Courier* had it.

After Brooklyn, Coup loaded the company on the railroad, and began the touring season. As we know, 1872 was the first season in which a special train was used to haul a complete circus. Because they used leased equipment that first year, there were many problems since the cars were not uniform. Coup saw to it that the flatcars were replaced by show-owned equipment in 1873. The trains had sixty-two to sixty-five cars of which fifty were Barnum's, the rest leased. The variation in numbers had to do with the various sizes of the cars provided by the individual railroads. There were five sleeping cars and six passenger cars in the make-up.

The route took them into New England, across New York to Buffalo, through Ohio, into Indiana and Illinois, coming up to Chicago, the furthest western point they reached. They played Chicago for a week, then went into Michigan, across Ontario, down to Washington and Baltimore, and a week in Philadelphia. Another week in Brooklyn ended the tenting portion of the route. They opened in the new Hippodrome building on October 20.

In some cities, Philadelphia and Cleveland among them, wooden amphitheatres with canvas roofs were constructed, foretelling the pattern to be followed by the Roman Hippodrome of 1874 and 1875. In Buffalo, anticipating large crowds, the show built some kind of gallery that increased seating by 3,000; details of this construction are so meagre it can't be described accurately. It is amazing that having increased the capacity by a third from the previous season, Coup now had to do even more.

RIGHT: Illustration cut line—purported parade view as printed in the 1873 *Barnum Courier*. The wagon at the top is the Temple of Juno, first used in 1871. The odd shaped one with strong verticals is the Polhymnia, a steam operated organ. At the bottom, the lion cage with band atop might be a fabrication, no specific reference to it being found.

All the important cities in the north were played. There were week-long stands in St. Louis, Chicago, Philadelphia and Brooklyn, ten days in Boston, and four-day stops in Cincinnati and Baltimore. There were three shows a day at 10 a.m., 1 p.m., and 7 p.m. Thus, there were 515 performances, plus or minus, in 1873, and it appears that the average audience was near to 9,700, three times the capacity of most circuses. Barnum wrote the business manager of the New York *Tribune* that it took audiences of 8,000 per day to cover the expenses.[4]

The comments in the press were supportive of the show, which is interesting, since it wasn't a fact twenty years before, at the time of the Barnum Caravan. His endeavors over the years seem to have solidified his image as essentially a man of good-will, but one who, perhaps, advertised himself to extremes. The Hartford *Courant* said, "There has been but one opinion expressed in Hartford about this monster combination. It is the universal expression that it more than fills public expectation. Surely nothing like it has ever before traveled through the country."[5] The Boston *Globe* printed, "We can only reiterate that it is the greatest exhibition of the kind that has ever visited Boston. The success which has met Mr. Barnum's efforts to give the public an exhibition which should be free from the objections so often brought against shows of this kind is an evidence that he has hit the public taste.[6] The Cleveland *Plain Dealer* pointed out that "Mr. Barnum has discovered the great secret of success. He has a remarkable show and he keeps it liberally advertised. Some people may think him extravagant, but "the proof of the pudding is in the eating," and his receipts, averaging ten thousand dollars a day, are an enduring proof of his wisdom in this particular."[7]

One unique addition to the lot layout was a 100 by 150 foot tent that was intended as a place for the public to rest while waiting for the performance to begin. Several cages of animals and a sideshow attraction or two were placed there, and no admission was charged. It closed when the front doors opened.

The operation was so efficient that only one performance was missed. This was the morning show in Lafayette, Indiana on July 30, and it was caused by a railroad accident ahead of the circus trains.

The parade in this season was enhanced by several additions, most of them being introduced for the first time on any circus. A band composed of black minstrels—not white men in blackface—paraded on the street, and were the concert attraction in the main show. A "Harmonium," as it was called, twenty-four feet long and seven feet wide, was a musical instrument, that must have been an imposing vehicle. Whatever its instrument was, it was worked with a small steam engine. The only word applied to musical chariots that a modern observer can grasp is "calliope." Words like "Harmonium," "Polyhymnia," and "Automatodean," tell us nothing, and, worse, do not distinguish between automatic machines and those operated by a person.

Barnum's parade had a Car of Juggernaut, and again we are not sure of what it was. It might have referred to the Temple of Juno, the telescoping throne chariot that was introduced in 1871. The bandwagon in 1873 was still the Chariot of Orpheus, and may have transported the minstrel band. A lion cage carried a band on the roof, at least such a combination was illustrated in the courier, which confirms the Troy *Times's* statement that there were two bands in the procession. Live bell-ringers rode on one of the museum wagons. All this enhancement of the parade can be credited to Howes' Great London Circus, which brought from England several truly innovative parade wagons (that had no other use or purpose) in 1871.

The Barnum parade took fifteen minutes to pass a given point, according to the Cleveland *Plain Dealer* of July 14. The order of march went: Grand chariot of Apollo bandwagon (formerly, chariot of Orpheus) with twelve-camel hitch—group of mounted knights in glittering armor and plumed helmets—group of mounted maidens, richly clad—group of Shetland ponies with child riders—mounted group, ladies in white and Robin Hood riders in green—two purple and gold cages, two-horse hitches—one large and three small elephants—large pink and silver lion cage, with automatodean on roof—twenty-nine cages, two-horse hitches—the harmonium, or polhymnia—a second group of cages—mammoth band car (identification unknown, possibly the lion cage)—snake den (glass) with hindu charmer inside—polar bear den—Chariot of the Sun (not identified)—museum chariots, mostly stuffed birds, with automatadia on roofs—Temple of Juno, thirty-feet high.[8]

There were three deaths in the company during the season. Edward D'Atalie, the thirty-three year-old "Man with the Iron Jaw," died in Fall River, Massachusetts on May 9, from an undisclosed illness. He was not what is called an iron-jaw performer today, that is, one who hangs by his teeth. D'Atalie lifted heavy objects by means of his mouth. His wife, Angela, performed with him, doing an act in which she fired a cannon from her shoulder. She continued this specialty in America for some years. On July 15, Charles Johnson, a property man, died in

Above: Orpheus Bandwagon, used by the show in 1871-73. Below: Either a cage or museum wagon (which look similar with sideboards up). As the wagon moved, a gearing system caused the flower to open and close and the figures to rotate.

Cleveland, from a stroke. A canvasman, George Lynch, was killed when run over by a stake wagon in St. Louis on August 3.

At season's end, the company moved into a building on the site of the later Madison Square Garden, between Madison and 4th Avenue, 26th and 27th Streets. It was there from October 20 to November 26, whereupon it moved into the American Institute building at Sixty-Third Street and Third Avenue. Capacity in this hall was 8,000 people.

The Barnum aggregation in 1873 was truly the greatest show on earth, in size, sales, income, and efficiency. Nothing like it had been offered the public in any prior season, and the public came to see it in droves. In Boston, in spite of a nine-day exposure, hundreds were turned away at each performance. Ticket sales were five times what they had been in 1872 (five million versus one million), and the profit was three times that of the previous year ($750,000 versus $280,000). These are obviously round numbers. The increases were partly because of the increase in seating from 10,000 to nearly 14,000, and partly because the route encompassed more large cities. In addition, it must be noted that 1872 was not a good year in the entertainment business. Under Coup's management the gross income had expanded two and a half times in 1872, and fifty per-cent above that in 1873 ($1.5 million versus $1 million).

The Indianapolis *News* editorialized on July 29:

> Barnum fools everybody for everybody is so accustomed to seeing big shows on the bulletin boards and small ones under canvas, that the opposite course astonishes and fools them.

With this reputation, and the great success that this season provided, it seems strange that the format of the traditional circus was abandoned for the following two seasons. Barnum was abroad for the last quarter of 1873, and, according to Saxon, the showman's chief biographer, had gathered many suggestions that were put into the Hippodrome presentation of 1874 and 1875. He had apparently had a long-cherished plan to exhibit a Roman Hippodrome, Zoological Institute, Aquaria, and Museum.[9]

A problem raised by the decision to embark on the Hippodrome project was the fate of the equipment, and the jobs of the personnel who were not needed in the new format. Barnum and Coup were never indifferent to their employees welfare, as they proved several times during the four-year reign of the circus. As for the equipment, it seems to have been too new and too valuable to sacrifice at auction prices. The solution arrived at was to lease the title and equipment to another showman, provided he engaged certain of the employees, and the presence of partner Hurd as treasurer.

John V. O'Brien of Frankford, Pennsylvania, a show owner of some ten years experience, was the man chosen to manage P. T. Barnum's Great Traveling Museum, Menagerie and World's Fair for the seasons of 1974 and 1875. He had with him Ed Tinkham as contracting agent; James Cooke, equestrian director; Horace Nichols, ringmaster; and W. L. Jukes, museum manager. Performers from the Barnum circus were Lucille Watson, George Donald, Jerry Hopper, Admiral Dot, the Fiji "cannibals," the Digger Indians, and the Circassian beauty. Dan Castello's trained horse, Senator, and his comic mules Pete and Barney, having no place with the Hippodrome, were part of O'Brien's lease, as were the museum wagons and many of the cages and their contents.

O'Brien maintained Barnum's two-ring format, but the biggest difference between the companies was that O'Brien's was a wagon show. Unfortunately for O'Brien the Panic of 1873 lasted until 1878, and not only was business bad, he lost $9,400 in the collapse of the Jay Gould bank. The lease ended on a sour note, and Barnum was forced to sue for a $14,000 shortfall.

It can only add to Barnum's place as the consumate showman that he would, after the most successful season, in terms of magnitude, of any circus in history, go in another direction. Further, it delineates him as being able to see beyond the circus, and to encompass spectacle for its own sake.

NOTES

[1] Saxon, p. 244.
[2] Barnum, *Struggles and Triumphs*, 1872 edition, p. 244.
[3] *P. T. Barnum's Advance Courier*, 1873.
[4] Letter, Barnum to Gordon L. Ford, April 24, 1873; Barnum, *Selected Letters*, p. 175.
[5] Hartford (CT) *Courant,* April 30, 1873.
[6] Boston (MA) *Globe,* May 22, 1873.
[7] Cleveland (OH) *Plain Dealer,* July 16, 1873.
[8] *Frank Leslie's Illustrated News,* July 12, 1873.
[9] Saxon, p. 246.

V
FORMATION OF P. T. BARNUM'S
GREAT ROMAN HIPPODROME, 1874

It was the morning of April 25, 1874. A grand parade, made up of valuable stock forwarded by P. T. Barnum from Europe, hit the streets of New York City, starting at 27th Street and proceeding to 26th, then to Third Avenue, to the Bowery, to Canal Street, to Broadway, to 14th Street, to Fifth Avenue, to 49th Street, to Madison Avenue, and ending at 27th Street where it began.

The procession was promoting the opening of P. T. Barnum's New Roman Hippodrome, which the newspaper advertisements were touting as "The Event of 1874," occupying an entire block bounded by Madison and Fourth Avenues and 26th and 27th Streets, "at an expense of nearly one million dollars"—the largest collection of living wild animals in the world, along with *The Congress of Nations*, described as "the most magnificent and dazzling spectacle ever witnessed in this country."[1]

A Roman Hippodrome? Not a circus? How could this be, when P. T. Barnum's Great Museum, Menagerie, Hippodrome and Traveling World's Fair, which was indeed a circus, had just the year before fulfilled a record-breaking summer tour? It is true that the 1873 Barnum show was the first traveling combination to include a hippodrome track within the main tent and to make use of it as part of the circus program. And the oval may have been used for limited races of some variety; but, as we have seen from the previous chapter, the route book gave no indication of them. More appropriately, the word "Hippodrome" in that title was indicative of the wooden seating oval within the enlarged pavilion. Nevertheless, the attention of the Barnum organization was now focused on a "non-circus"

Hippodromic races as spectator entertainment were not new to America in 1874. They were introduced some twenty-one years earlier by a syndicate of eight investors which included circus and menagerie notables Avery Smith, Richard Sands, Lewis B. Titus, and Seth B. Howes, with a troupe brought to this country, including the famous

French equestrian proprietor, Henri Franconi. The site selected was on the northwest corner of 23rd Street and Broadway. Formerly occupied by Corporal Thompson, it had been a popular resort of refreshment and conviviality, particularly noted as a stopping place for turfmen and others in the sport of trotting horses. After the land was acquired from the Howland estate, the hostelry was torn down and replaced by a building covering about two acres of ground to house the exhibition of mock chariot races and other gladiatorial events.

The new structure was erected from designs supplied by Mons. Franconi, after whose name the place was dedicated. The exterior was formed by brick walls two stories high. The auditorium was covered with a tin roof, and the arena area with green and white striped canvas. The whole appearance was described as "turreted abutments decorated with classic carvings, and capped with grotesque ornaments." The interior, as one might expect, was in the form of an oval measuring 300 feet in length and 200 feet in width, similar in size to the 1873 Barnum main pavilion. The hippodrome track was 1,000 feet in circumference, the infield of which was decorated with shrubs, illuminated fountains and other ornamentations, and the whole lighted by 1,000 gas jets. Seating was arranged into seven tiers forming a capacity of anywhere from 4,000 to 10,000 people, depending on which source one accepts.[2]

Since the Franconi affair, the use of the word "hippodrome" to describe a place of exhibition or form of entertainment appears on occasion in circus advertising; but there is nothing to suggest from this that any form of actual racing occurred around a hippodrome track. As has already been stated, the Barnum show of 1873 was the first circus with a canvas large enough to accommodate such a feature.[3]

An exception to this took place indoors across the country in San Francisco, where, on the site of the old Mechanics Pavilion, John Wilson's Hippodrome, was attracting audiences in 1865. The place was arranged with two rings, an inner and outer one. In the larger, all sorts of races were contested—hurdle, chariot, Roman, pony, and even running. The smaller ring was used for Ella Zoyara's principal act on horseback, for Painter and Durand's *la perche equipoise*, for exhibition of the trained colt, Othello, and for other gymnastic and acrobatic activities. Several events were featured during the short season. A number of hose companies vied for championship of the mile run around the oval track. And pacing and trotting horse races were offered with purses amounting to $100 and $250. This venture was within a permanent

Franconi's Hippodrome, Madison Square, New York
[*Gleason's Pictorial Drawing-Room Companion*, June 25, 1853]

Interior Franconi's Hippodrome [*Gleason's Pictorial Drawing-Room Companion*, June 25, 1853]

structure and of a short life. The population of California at that time was not of sufficient numbers to support lengthy engagements.

The idea for Barnum's New Roman Hippodrome must have been his own. In his autobiography he referred to a "long-cherished plan of exhibiting a Roman Hippodrome, Zoological Institute, Aquaria, and Museum of unsurpassing extent and magnificence."[4] Coup and Hurd had shown in the past they were much too cautious to propose such an expensive venture. Barnum revealed that when preparations were being made for the 1872 tenting season, Coup expressed "great agony" over the large sums of money being expended for animals and other items. And Hurd concurred that "the season would prove ruinous" unless Barnum agreed to sell off some of his expensive purchases.[5] In contrast, Barnum's propensity for "bigness," for topping his previous achievements, for a seeming enjoyment of public acknowledgment, and, yes, because of the financial success of the 1873 tenting season, all supported the daring of such a scheme. In a letter to Gordon L. Ford, Barnum justified the move in the following manner:[6]

> I felt a great *desire* to do a *big thing* for the public & to make it quite unobjectionable to the most refined & moral. I think I have succeeded. It is my last "crowning effort." Three months of the same success which I am now receiving (pecuniarily) will be required in order to reimburse the outlays made since last November. The present excitement must wane before that time, I think, but in *time* I have no doubt of getting my money back. But whether so or not is of less consequence than the fact that I have awakened a *public taste* which *will not* henceforth be satisfied with namby-pamby nonsense. Managers will be *required* hereafter to give their patrons something *better* & therein is the public benefited, and I am satisfied.

This, at the age sixty-three, was to be his last hurrah, elevating, free of all objectionable features and appealing to the patronage of the most moral and refined classes—the ultimate and lasting gemstone to adorn the Barnum public image. There is no indication how early in 1873 the plans for this last "crowning effort" were set in motion. We know of Barnum's decision to make a visit to Europe in September to, as he stated in his autobiography, "run over and see the International Exhibition at Vienna."[7] But, whenever, the commitment to organize a huge hippodrome entertainment was made before he left the country.

After attending the fair and traveling to Berlin, the news was received from his representatives—W. C. Coup and S. H. Hurd—that the New York and Harlem Railroad Company property at Fourth Avenue and Twenty-sixth Street could be leased. This probably coincided with the period in November when the Barnum circus had moved onto the property for a brief time. The site was said to be the only vacant grounds in New York City large enough to accommodate the hippodrome Barnum envisioned. It had been rented to various parties after the station was abandoned and the place deserted with the opening of Grand Central Station at 42nd Street in 1871. Barnum immediately wired back the go-ahead for the tract to be secured.

When the circus left for the American Institute building at the end of November it may have been to allow the renovations to occur. Several brick buildings were removed and the whole block between Fourth and Madison was utilized for the erection of a large frame placed within the shell of the existing main structure, the whole to be styled somewhat after the manner of the ancient Roman amphitheatre and, one might add, similar to the previous Franconi coliseum, with a projected joint seating capacity of 16,000 people.

It can be noted that there was early opposition to the erection of the Hippodrome through complaints made at a meeting of the Assistant Board of Aldermen. Present at that time were Messrs. Rankin, Fellows, and Thornell, representing the Board of Underwriters' Association, and a number of property owners within the vicinity of the old railroad site. There was general fear of a potential for fire within that thickly-settled portion of the city from such a construction. Chief Engineer Bates of the Fire Department, who was also in attendance, concurred that in the event of a conflagration a large portion of the city could be endangered. Representatives of the Underwriters' Association warned that few insurance companies would take risks on the property. Wherewith, Barnum's agent informed the gathering that two companies had already agreed to do so.[8]

In typical political fashion, a committee was appointed, consisting of Messrs. Codington, Kreps, and Cumiski, to look into the matter and submit a report. On February 10, members of said committee and a number of property owners inspected the site, the building being in the process of erection, and came away with the conclusion that indeed the construction created possibilities of fire that could endanger life and surrounding property. While the four walls were of brick, the seats and roof were erected of timber, some of which was old and unreliable. And with its large seating capacity—not the 16,000 that had been envisioned—

fire during a performance could create a dangerous condition of panic amongst the gathered auditory.

The Committee of Assistant Aldermen held another meeting on February 16 to report on their examination of the building. Barnum's representative informed the Committee that there were to be twelve or fourteen large doors for egress in case of fire or panic, that no fire or heaters were to be used in the building; gas was to be installed but all the wood-work near the gas burners were to be covered with tin. There would be hydrants placed in various location and a sufficient quantity of hose at hand for use if needed. Two main doors, fifteen feet wide, would be capable of allowing the entrance of two fire engines abreast. As it turned out, there were two commodious entrances—one on Fourth Avenue and another in the middle of the block on Madison. The exits numbered eighteen, so arranged that, by estimate, the building could be emptied in five to ten minutes.

The committee members, in their wisdom, found that the building was safe from the danger of fire and had much better opportunity for egress than other places of amusements. So stated, they offered the belated opinion that they, as a committee of Assistant Aldermen, had no jurisdiction in the matter and, therefore, respectfully asked to be discharged from further consideration.[9] So much for community opposition.

News of the construction drew considerable discussion in the local press. An item stated that a special survey had been made of the premises at the instigation of the Mayor, the results of which indicated that the plans and work were in strict accordance with the building law. Then George B. Butler of the Union League Club, protesting against its completion, called upon the Mayor to remove the Superintendent of Buildings "if he shall refuse to stop the further erection of [the] edifice on the original plan, or upon any plan which subjects the city to danger." Whereupon the Superintendent of Public Buildings made a new survey of the structure and gave orders to the builders that important changes needed to be made, otherwise he would enjoin the work. Work was then suspended while the proprietors took the matter under consideration.[10]

Meanwhile, Barnum was fast at work. He claims to have visited all the zoological gardens, circuses, and public exhibitions wherever he went—the Paris Hippodrome Paris, Circus Renz at Vienna, Myers' Circus at Dresden, Silamonski and Carré's Circus at Cologne, Zoological

Gardens at Hamburg, Amsterdam and other Continental cities—thereby acquiring various novelties and valuable ideas. By November 18, he had purchased nearly a "ship load" of birds and animals at Hamburg.

He then moved on to England where on January 2 he contracted with John and George Sanger to purchase duplicates of the entire wardrobe and paraphernalia connected with the pageant of *The Congress of Monarchs*. This spectacle had been exhibited at Agricultural Hall, London, some years earlier. The Sangers had surfaced to prominence there through a series of expensive productions, the first being this particular piece. Nothing so extravagant had ever been done in London previously, and so successful was it that upwards of 37,000 people were said to have attended in a single day.

The Sangers were well rewarded. For the sum of £33,000, Barnum received the full list of chariots, costumes, trappings, flags, banners, etc.—£13,000 to be paid in advance, the remainder at the fulfillment of the terms of the contract.[11] This was confirmed by W. C. Coup in his *Sawdust and Spangles*. He stated that *The Congress of Nations* cost "Mr. Barnum and myself" over $40,000. In George Sanger's memoirs, however, the figure given was £25,000.[12]

The operating staff for the Hippodrome company was much the same as the preceding years. P. T. Barnum as the nominal proprietor was assisted by William C. Coup, Dan Castello, and Samuel H. Hurd. Coup was general manager and Castello "director of amusements." These men had proven their worth within the Barnum organization over the last three years. As Coup stated, "As far as the technical details of the show are concerned, Mr. Barnum was absolutely ignorant."[13] They had instigated at least two important elements that contributed to the show's immense success—creative use of rail travel and the addition of a second ring, thereby solving the problem of audience viewing within an expanding canvas while at the same time increasing the seating capacity.[14]

Hurd worked under the title of superintendent and treasurer. Having married Barnum's oldest daughter, Helen, in the fall of 1857, his connection with the Barnum management began as early as 1864 when he was listed as an assistant for the second American Museum. Although the couple were divorced in 1871, Barnum maintained a trust in the ex-son-in-law to look after his financial interests. Indeed, Hurd had been promoted from assistant treasurer to treasurer for the 1872 season.

Henri Franconi and Horse Bayard, Opening Night

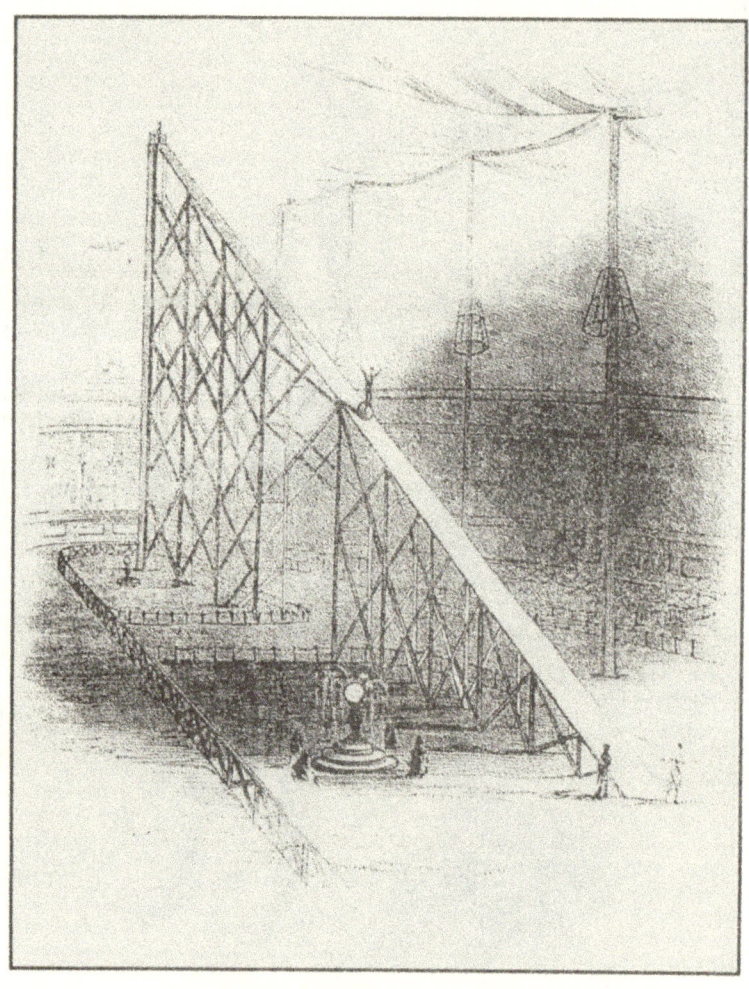

Franconi's Hippodrome, New York
A Man Ascends on a Large Ball at a Height of Forty Feet
[*Illustrated News*, June 11, 1853]

Charles W. Fuller, a man of wide experience, was the general agent. As far back as 1853, he was connected with Franconi's Hippodrome. In the interim there were engagements with Rivers & Derious, 1854-55; James W. Myers', 1856; Nixon & Kemp, 1856-57; James M. Nixon's, 1859-60; S. O. Wheeler's, 1863; and L. B. Lent's, 1864, 1867-72. In 1865, as proprietor of the Monitor Show, he traveled with a wagon fashioned after the gunboat of that name, containing a stereopticon and panoramic views of the Civil War.

David S. Thomas was the press agent. He had been with Dan Rice's Paris Pavilion Circus in 1871, during which time Louis E. Cooke credits him with being the first of his breed to travel back with the show and devote full time to entertaining newspapermen. He would continue working under the Barnum circus banner, and deservedly so, well into the 1880s.

We find it interesting that James M. Nixon was engaged to assist Castello in directing the hippodromic events. Castello had formerly performed with Nixon's circus in the summer of 1859 through the eastern states and Canada as principal clown, along with Don Juan, his educated bull. The year of 1866 marked the beginning of an association between the two men when they put out a show under the Dan Castello title—Castello as the drawing card and Nixon as manager. The relationship continued for the next three years and, with the opening of the transcontinental railroad, the showmen routed their circus from the eastern coast to the Pacific Ocean.

Nixon's association with P. T. Barnum went back many years. The two were connected in management in 1860 when they erected a tent at Broadway and Thirteenth Street, New York City, in which to house Grizzly Adams' California Menagerie. Within the tent were displayed a variety of western wild life, with the Adams trained grizzlies demonstrating their agility and their versatility through singing, climbing, dancing, vaulting, and somersaulting. In July of that year Barnum and Nixon combined to take Cooke's Royal Circus with Old Grizzly Adams California Menagerie on tour.

Acquiring Nixon to assist with the Roman Hippodrome was a wise choice. Although Castello came into this with some years of experience as an equestrian director, his requisites for developing dramatic spectacle were far inferior to Nixon's. It appears to the authors that, although Barnum supplied the grand scheme for the Roman Hippodrome, Nixon's hand at bringing it off was far more instrumental than he has heretofore been given credit. In support of this, some examples of former activities might be useful.

James M. Nixon had worked his way from a mere groom with Aaron Turner's circus around 1836 to performing with various troupes in the 1840s and 1850s as acrobat, ringmaster and equestrian director. In 1849 he became manager for Crane & Co.'s Great Oriental Circus where, the advertisements informed us: "The establishment on entering town will be preceded by the Monster Dragon Chariot, drawn by Ten Camels Of the Syrian breed, lately imported from the Deserts of Arabia for Crane & Company." One might note that the closing number of the show's program was a set of miniature hippodrome races, put on entirely with ponies and juvenile equestrians, a sort of burlesque sporting scene entitled *The Pony Races*.[15]

With the opening of Franconi's Hippodrome, Nixon was employed as its equestrian director, supervising races of various kinds and pageantries such as *The Field of the Cloth of Gold*, in which men dressed as knights presented mock battles. For the winter season of 1857-58, he was equestrian director for John Tryon's New National Circus, 84 Bowery, where during the run the spectacle of *Cinderella* was produced under his supervision.

Nixon became the full lessee of Niblo's Garden, where he opened a circus under the title of "Cooke's Equestrian Troupe from Astley's Royal Amphitheatre, London," on January 16, 1860. The Nixon designed entertainment included a very attractive opening scene, presented with the entire troupe appearing on the stage in the various characters representing the exercises within a piece called *The Oriental Festival*—a procession of lanterns, the feats of a troupe of acrobats, the tricks of several conjurers with knives, balls, plates, etc., and finally a series of ballet dances. In addition to his involvement with the so-called Cooke troupe, Nixon was the house proprietor at Niblo's, where between circus visits he was still responsible for keeping the place going—booking burlesques, vaudevilles and comediettas, as well as operating the gardens with its rainbow of finely decorated flowers, spacious and magnificent arbors and botanical and aquaria exhibits.

The same troupe returned to Niblo's on April 9 and began offering a series of spectacles. A new version of *The Bronze Horse*, with musical and dramatic features and an equine ascension as a grand climax, was extremely well received. There followed *Merry Sports of England* and *Blue Beard*. The engagement terminated on May 26 with

Cinderella, enacted almost entirely by children. Then, after completing a short summer tour, the circus moved back into Niblo's where the historical pageant, *The Oriental Festival*, was restored; also the equestrian spectacle, *The Field of the Cloth of Gold*, presented in tandem with *The Steeple-Chase; or Life in Merry England*.

In the spring of 1862, Nixon took a lease on Palace Gardens in New York City and converted and enlarged it into a place of Elysian beauty similar to the Cremorne Gardens of London. He developed three new features on the property—a stretch of canvas under which equestrian performances were given; a building devoted to the display of trees, flowers and shrubbery called Floral Hall; and a concert pagoda designated the Palace of Music; all in all, an intermingling of natural beauty, ballet, opera, and circus. During this Nixon managed project, the pantomimes *Spirit of the Flood*, *The Golden Egg*, and *The Wizard Skiff* were presented in turn.

Still another major Nixon endeavor was the opening on February 8, 1864, of a structure modeled after the *Champs Élysées* in Paris. Described as "the new and superb equestrian temple," the place was designated the Hippotheatron. An interesting feature was the use of two ring entrances stationed opposite each other, which allowed utility and flexibility for *battoute* leaping and the staging of spectacles. His company occupied the place for two winter seasons, during which the pantomimes of *Harlequin Bluebeard*, *Harlequin Mother Goose*, *The Fairy Prince O'Donohue*, and *The Elixir of Life, or, the Birth of Harlequin* were produced.

Elements of this brief biographic within Nixon's lengthy career have been selected to illustrate his experience in creating and staging ring entertainments, which far exceeded that of his administrative colleagues connected with the hippodrome project. The rationale for his employment, then, extended beyond mere friendship with Dan Castello; it is apparent he had much to offer as "assistant director." In addition to his artistic contributions, he had the responsibility of giving the signal for starting the races, striking the warning bell for the homestretch, and deciding who were the victors—a combination of judge, bailiff and jury. The *Clipper* expressed its approval with: "James M. Nixon, the veteran circus manager, discharges his arduous duties as superintendent with an easy grace and the utmost fairness."[16]

The finished Hippodrome was built of brick, iron, glass and wood. There was a solid roof extending from the outer walls over the

"P. T. Barnum as the Modern Gulliver," by caricaturist E. Jump, depicting the great showman seated atop the ruins of the old New Haven depot listening to the remonstrances of the Lilliputians against the erection of his Hippodrome upon the site.
[New York *Clipper*, March 21, 1874]

seating area. The covering or canopy above the performing space, eighty feet in width, consisted of light waterproof canvas, manufactured for the purpose in the style of an Italian pavilion, with alternate stripes of rich and variegated colors. Six wooden spars nearly one hundred feet in height were the main support of the flexible roof—each one, projecting through it, festooned with flags. The inner posts, some twenty in number, supporting the permanent, slate-roofed portion were decorated with shields and flags of different nations. In all, the structure measured 427 by 200 feet. The track was thirty-five feet wide at the ends and twenty-six at the sides, with a total circumference of one-fifth mile.[17]

As one passed through the main entrance on Madison Avenue, the whole length of the right side of the building, beneath the tiered seating, served as the menagerie—penned animals on the right of the passage and cages on the left. On the Twenty-Seventh Street corner was a large aquarium. The left side of the structure was occupied as stables for the ring stock.

The family circle, on the Twenty-Sixth Street side, was furnished with benches covered by carpeting; the gallery, on the Fourth Avenue side, with plain seating; the parquet, on the Twenty-Seventh Street side, with cane-bottom chairs; the orchestra section, extending nearly the full length of one side, with patent iron folding chairs. Four sumptuous private boxes, accommodating eight people each, were located near the Madison Avenue entrance. On the opposite side were "retiring rooms for ladies, supplied with all the necessary assistants for toilet arrangement."[18] Recognizing the concerns of the civic authorities, the cement-floored promenade encircling the auditory was spacious and equipped with huge iron doors by which, in case of fire, the flames could be confined to a single compartment.

A large area in the center of the arena, surrounded by the hippodrome track, was enclosed with a light railing. A roadway was placed through it, branching at either end into two entrances. On both sides of this were grassy plots supporting an abundance of flowers. At each end of the arena was a fountain of running water; midway there was a music stand; and somewhere was located a pond where "graceful swans disport[ed] at ease." Between each post, suspended from the roof, were mechanical birds, made in Paris, which issued forth sweet chirping sounds as the audience was being ushered to their seats.[19] For lighting, there were chandeliers over this enclosure, augmented by two rows of gas lights around the track and seating area. The entrance through which the various processions and chariots entered to the scene of action, located at the easterly, or Fourth Avenue, end of the interior, was thirty feet high and twenty feet wide.

The construction was completed on April 1, 1874. The original opening was set for the evening of Thursday, April 23, but was delayed because of last minute complications. Finally, as banners waved their welcome atop the canvas roof, the opening night patrons crowded their way into the huge structure to bear witness to this gala event; but they would not celebrate the presence of the star attraction—Barnum was still at sea, a few days shy of New York harbor.

NOTES

[1] New York *Times*, April 24, 1874.

[2] Saxon, "Franconi in America," p. 13.

[3] The first to use "Hippodrome" in the title of an American circus was Dan Rice in 1852-54, but there was no hippodrome track. Others were Levi J. North, June & Co., and Rufus Welch, 1853; H. C. Lee, 1854. The true originator was Victor Franconi in Paris, copied by Batty in London.

[4] Barnum, *Struggles and Triumphs*, 1927 edition, p. 691.

[5] Saxon, *P. T. Barnum*, p. 239-240.

[6] P. T. Barnum, *Selected Letters*, p. 181.

[7] Barnum, *Struggles and Triumphs*, op. cit., p. 690. On the other hand, in a letter to Joseph Henry sent from Bridgeport and dated September 19 [Barnum, *Selected Letters*, p. 177], Barnum indicated his European trip was to investigate the possibility of sending a balloon across the Atlantic. He claimed a long-time interest in aerial navigation and was at this time prepared to consult with authorities in England and France and to put up the money for such a flight. [New York *Times*, September 18, 1873]. The bottom line being, a successful project of this nature could show profitable returns by merely exhibiting the balloon, not to mention the balloonist.

[8] New York *Times*, February 11, 1874.

[9] Loeffler, "A Re-Examination of the History of Madison Square Garden (etc.)," p. 9.

[10] New York *Clipper*, February 14, 1874.

[11] Barnum, *Struggles and Triumphs*, pp. 691-696.

[12] George Sanger, *Seventy Years a Showman*, p. 158.

[13] New York *Clipper*, May 16, 1891.

[14] Castello claimed that Barnum came to him with the question: "What are we going to do? The canvas is getting so big that the people can't see." "We'll put in two rings," was Castello's reply. [clipping, "A Nestor of Clown,"

Syracuse *Standard*, 1899.] It is more likely that the idea came from a discussion amongst the principals involved.

[15] Charles Bernard, "Old-Time Showmen," p. 64.
[16] New York *Clipper*, June 6, 1874.
[17] *Frank Leslie's Illustrated Newspaper*, May 9, 1874.
[18] *Ibid.*
[19] *Ibid.*

P. T. Barnum's Roman Hippodrome [New York *Graphic*, March 5, 1874]

VI
FIRST NEW YORK ENGAGEMENT OF BARNUM'S ROMAN HIPPODROME, 1874

When the Hippodrome opened to the public on April 27, the list of officialdom read as follows: P. T. Barnum, proprietor; W. C. Coup, general manager; S. H. Hurd, superintendent and treasurer; B. S. Kellogg, assistant treasurer; Dan Castello, director of amusements; James M. Nixon, superintendent of amusements; Frank Whittaker, assistant superintendent of amusements; C. W. Fuller, general agent; D. S. Thomas, press agent; F. A. Bartlett, superintendent of excursions; Dr. L. B. Woods, purchasing agent; Prof. Franz Hartzman, musical director.

Commentary in the New York *Herald* suggested that 15,000 New Yorkers created a crush never before been seen at any public place of amusement in the city since the days of Ellen Tree or Fanny Ellsler at the old Park Theatre. The jam was so great, it stated, that the police were almost powerless—although at times exercised their clubs vigorously upon the hats and heads of the surging crowd—and a number of ladies fainted under the pressure of the pushing and shoving multitude.[1]

The press was invited to a dress rehearsal prior to the opening and a large number of prominent citizens were guests of the proprietors to preview the well publicized event. The special run-through had been scheduled for Wednesday, April 22, but was postponed until Friday because, while Nixon was sitting in a chariot observing an earlier rehearsal, a horse smashed into it, leaving the equestrian director severely injured. But by Friday he was able to conduct his duties with an arm well bandaged and frayed nerves suitably becalmed. However, his associate, Dan Castello, was home sick with pneumonia. And P. T. Barnum had not returned from Europe.

From newspaper accounts of the evening, we learn that the program opened with a brilliant pageant entitled *The Congress of Nations*, which was a show in itself, bearing no relationship to the rest of the program. It took the place of the old-fashioned *grand entrée*. The huge procession around the hippodrome track consisted of magnificent chariots and tableaux cars and long lines of court retainers and soldiers,

Hippodrome Interior [*Frank Leslie's Illustrated Newspaper*, May 9, 1874]

mounted and on foot, in which many of the courts of Europe and the East were represented—Great Britain, France, Germany, Russia, Italy, the Vatican, China, Turkey, Ireland, India, Egypt, and the United States. The theme reflected a nineteenth century passion for world discovery—a curiosity about not only ancient cultures but of existing ones as well, both human and animal. The founding of zoological gardens and the popularity of touring menageries were a part of this. But perhaps more profoundly, the great world exhibitions, which had been occurring with frequency in the latter half of the nineteenth century, included cottages within which individual nations defined themselves. The most recent, the Vienna Exhibition of 1873, which we know Mr. Barnum attended, may have influenced this particular choice for the opening spectacle.

First in the procession was England, moving to the music of "God Save the Queen," and represented by an entry of heralds followed by knights bearing the national standard. Then came the royal carriage, on which the likeness of Queen Victoria sat comfortably enthroned, accompanied by her maids of honor, and surrounded by an escort of Life Guards, Grenadiers, Highlanders, and knights in full armor—some of them supposedly past monarchs of the realm from William the Conqueror to Edward the Black Prince, all dressed in costumes historically correct.

France was next, with horsemen representing Napoleon I and his generals, accompanied by an escort of the Imperial Guard and a unit of Zouaves. After this entered the Cross Keys of the Holy See, borne by a standard bearer and followed by seven guards. His Holiness the Pope entered on a chariot shielded by eight members of the College of Cardinals and followed by a deputation of Bishops. The German contingent consisted of a company of Prussian soldiers, the Kaisers Wilhelm, Bismarck, and Von Moltke being on horseback and accompanied by imperial escorts. This was followed by the "Sublime Porte," with a staff mounted on Arabian steeds and "shimmering with Oriental splendor," trailed by a chariot carrying a half-dozen ladies of the harem, protected by slaves and a body of troops. Italy was next, represented by a number of sharpshooters, Il Re Galantuomo and his staff, and a company of Garibaldians. The Pasha of Egypt was seen in a chariot leading six ladies mounted on camels and guarded by Egyptian soldiers. The Czar of Russia followed in the procession with his staff and armed detachment of Cossack and Circassian guard. The Irish contingent, with its body of ancient warriors and boys of the shamrock, marched around to "The

Wearing of the Green." Spain was represented by Columbus and his attendants, Queen Isabella and her Court and a number of bull fighters. Then came the Empress of China, reclining in a dragon car, accompanied by mandarins and the great sage, Confucious. India was next in line, with richly dressed groups of men and women representing the Sultan and his favorites, with attending Sepoys, Hindoos, etc., and three ladies mounted on elephants. The Stars and Stripes brought up the rear to the strains of "Hail, Columbia," followed by men in the garb of settlers, a body of Revolutionary militia, a company of United States infantry, and a tribe of Indians. This ended an impressive opening.[2]

Great pains were taken to make the impersonators of national figures as representative as possible. Coup stated years later in an interview with a newspaper man that the management spent "thousands of dollars" to get people who resembled the originals. He recalled that William H. Vanderbilt commissioned a painting of Horace F. Clark, the man who was cast as Napoleon, which he hung in his gallery with "Napoleon" as the title. The Kaiser Wilhelm was a German nobleman Coup found in a barber shop and paid fifteen dollars a week for donning a helmet and riding around the track twice a day.[3]

There is no doubt but that the spectacle was breathtaking to an 1874 audience. It was repeatedly described by observers in such phrases as "huge gilded cars," "gorgeously mounted chariots," "splendidly caparisoned camels, elephants, horses, and ponies," and "hundreds of performers in elegant costumes." The elaborate procession would draw awestruck attention from audience and press during its New York run and, in the future, wherever the show was presented.

The *grand entrée* was supervened by a series of races and variety performances. There was flat racing between men mounted on English thoroughbreds, racing between men standing astride two horses, Roman two-horse chariots racing, English jockey racing, hurdle racing and, let us not fail to mention, elephant, monkey, and ostrich racing. There was also a liberty race between some twenty horses without riders or harness. At the end of each of the heats, the victor was handed a flag, who then made a circle around the course to receive the approbation of the audience.

We have found nothing to indicate that these contests were fixed or staged in any deceptive way. It appears that each equestrian and equestrienne put forth a winning effort at every encounter. The struggle of horse and human to best the field was intense, so much so that there

were frequent injuries. In fact, the New York *Times* reported later "that several people [had] been killed there." This charge was denied by a Hippodrome representative.[4]

    A moment of levity occurred at this dress rehearsal during the ostrich event. When two men on horseback attempted to encourage three ostriches around the track by waving red flags, one of the feathered racers, seemingly unwilling to compete, slipped between the riders and trotted along after them, much preferring the role of spectator. As one would expect, the audience of guests and media people expressed their enjoyment of the unfolding skit. There were also interludes of intended humor. A bit of satirical fun was offered when "Mme. Pompadour's

Carriage in Central Park" was represented by a double turnout carrying a dozen dignified monkeys. There was also a comical race between a half-dozen such primates mounted on ponies.

In between the races there were various specialty acts. Most of these were the type that could be executed above ground level to allow the vast auditory adequate vantage. Performers who were not mounted on horses were brought into the arena in an elegant barouche with a coachman and footman in livery and introduced by being driven once around the arena. Millson & Lazelle performed on a trapeze, terminating with leaps to a single rope some distance away. Mons. Joignerey juggled cannon balls and lifted two ponies some four or five inches from the ground while hanging by his feet from a trapeze. Mons. Loyal performed his aerial specialty on the triple trapeze as well. Signor Leonchi, dressed as an Indian, demonstrated his skill with a lasso while mounted on horseback. The program terminated with a chariot race between Mme. D'Atalie, driving four black horses abreast, engaged against Mons. Arnaud behind a team of four white ones. Although the above is a description of a complimentary performance, succeeding audiences could witness this same display for the admission price in the grand orchestra of $1.50; the orchestra, $1; the balcony, 75¢; family circle, 50¢; gallery, 25¢; or a private box holding eight, $8.

A number of adjustments within the program were made rather quickly. In the two-horse chariot race, it was found that the track width was too narrow to allow three contestants to run abreast during the excitement of the contest, so one chariot was eliminated. The amount of riders in the flat and hurdle races was also reduced to give them more room and to diminish the possibility of accidents occurring. This particularly effected the equestriennes, since a few of them had been thrown and somewhat injured. And, perhaps because of the dress rehearsal high jinks, the ostrich race was abandoned for the time being.[5]

From all accounts the new hippodrome was off to a flourishing start. The people crowding into this large arena adversely affected business at other establishments of entertainment. Advertisements claimed an average daily attendance of 20,000, with thousands unable to gain admission for the evening performances.[6] This may have been an overstatement; but the place, which on completion seated somewhere between 10,000 and 12,000 spectators, was reported to have been filled nightly. Barnum wrote in his autobiography that the Hippodrome had provision for 10,000 and that "for weeks in succession all the best seats were engaged days in advance," and that every evening performance "thousands were turned away."⁷ At the daily matinees, however, although well attended, one could easily obtain seating. To increase daytime business, the Barnum management made arrangements for the operation of excursion trains from the surrounding communities within a radius of some two hundred miles. This was successful in bringing in large numbers of ruralites. Advertisements repeatedly promised that the Hippodrome was "the coolest summer resort in the city." The purchase of tickets was made easy by keeping the boxoffice open from 8:00 a.m. to 4:00 p.m., where seats could be secured four days in advance. Tickets were also available at Millet & Co., 437 Broadway.

April 30th marked the arrival from Liverpool of P. T. Barnum on the steamer *Scotia*. That night he attended his great dream for the first time. Once the audience became aware of his presence, they were enthusiastic in calling him out. He then stepped into the barouche and, standing hat in hand, was driven around the arena to cheers of welcome and resounding applause. As one might expect, he termed that night "the greatest assemblage of people ever gathered in one building in New York." And added that his "enthusiastic reception was at once a testimonial of the public appreciation of one of [his] greatest efforts in [his] managerial career, and a verdict that it was a complete and gratifying success."⁸

After only a few weeks into the run, novelties were being added to the program. Among these was ostrich herding and riding. The three ostriches, perhaps to make amends for their earlier misconduct, were driven around the arena by small boys waving red flags, a scene of additional mirth in the absence of clowns.

A new sequence was put in place, consisting of Leonchi's Tribe of Indians and Mexican Rangers, within which various "scenes of Indian life" could be observed—preparing a camp on the plains, a buffalo hunt by six young chiefs, the mistreatment of a white prisoner, a Canadian snow shoe race, a hurdle race by six young braves on their ponies, a hurdle foot race by twelve young men, "Deerfoot's" race against a horse, and the "Chase for a Wife."

The inclusion of "Deerfoot" was not happenstance. Indian runners were well recognized for their speed and endurance in competitions by the middle of the nineteenth century. One of these, a Seneca named Lewis Bennett, but called "Deerfoot," emerged as a formidable contender. In the early 1860s a British promoter brought him to England, where his racing achievements made him a celebrity. He returned to this country during the Civil War and continued to compete. At this time, 1874, he was forty-four years old, still running but generally as a novelty at fairs, competing against horses. It remains a question as to whether or not the "Deerfoot" with the Hippodrome was the genuine article. On one hand, "Deerfoot" was active at this time; but, on the other, if it were the real Seneca, why was it that the Barnum people did not take greater advantage of his celebrity?

In "Chase for a Wife" the chief's daughter was placed on a swift horse and pursued by her suitors. According to Indian custom (or at least custom *a la* Barnum), she would become the wife of the brave who captured her. Flying from her pursuers, she assumed various athletic positions in which she seemed to scarcely touch her horse while riding at top speed. The chase consisted of several Indian warriors, including Leonchi, the famous Mexican hunter. The men pursued the princess at a lightning pace until, finally, she was overtaken by Leonchi, who clasped his arms around her, lifted her from her pony to his own while at full gallop, and carried her triumphantly into camp.

There was also an act called "The Indian Mazeppa." While swiftly circling the track, a rider attired in Mexican costume picked up handkerchiefs left at various locations. After a captured Indian was tied to the bare back of a horse, justifying the "Mazeppa" in the title, the aforementioned rider pursued him and, throwing a lasso around the horse's neck, brought the animal to a stop.

Added to the non-riding acts were Satsuma and Little All Right, who performed their Japanese ladder balancing act. Charles White, who had been with the Barnum show since 1872, entered a den of performing lions as the big cage was pulled around the oval by a four-horse team to allow vantage from the whole of the arena.[9]

Mlle. Victoria, "The Queen of the Lofty Wire," whose evasive last name is unknown to us, made her debut on the afternoon of May 25. This young lady, "not yet on the shady side of twenty years," was a native of England. She had been performing since the age of five or six; and, previous to her coming to the United States on the urging of Barnum, had been well received on the Continent. One of her daring ventures at that time was to cross the river Seine on a tight-rope.

At the Hippodrome she walked across a wire suspended between two pillars. She then re-crossed it while her head was enveloped in a sack, and again riding on a velocipede, the wheels of which were deeply grooved to fit the rope. A balance pole was used in every feat. The act was deemed only "fair" by a *Clipper* observer: "Her performance may have been surpassed in this country by Blondin, Harry Leslie, John Denier, Mlle. Zanfretta, Marietta Ravel, and numerous others, all of whom perform without a balance-pole."[10]

At the outset, Mlle. Victoria's performances were limited to daily matinees and Monday and Friday evenings, "owing to immense strain on the physical and mental system."[11] By the week of June 8, her stamina had increased, perhaps through boxoffice necessity; for she began appearing at all matinee and evening performances on a wire that had been both raised and lengthened.

There were more novelties during the week. Contestants who were termed "metropolitan amateurs" vied for victory in the sack and wheelbarrow races. A carriage was on display purported to have once belonged to the Lord Mayor of London, and last used by ex-Emperor Napoleon III. The rest of the program was much the same as previous weeks. A salient feature was the Roman standing race, with Benjamin Stevens, William Hoyle, and George North, erect and astride two horses each. Mme. D'Atalie was still racing in her chariot, but the male opponent had been replaced by Ella Grady.[12]

Another charioteer, a Miss Mattie Lewis, was seriously injured during the night performance of June 15. After winning her race and starting off the track, another driver's horse crashed into her chariot, pinning her against the side. Although bruised severely, she reappeared a few days later, but was forced to retire for a time because of internal bleeding.

During the week of June 22 a mammoth black rhinoceros was added to the menagerie department. This specimen was said to weigh 9,500 pounds, being some 2,000 pounds heavier than the rhino at the Zoological Gardens, London.[13] Also at this time a new advertising piece was issued, a pamphlet small enough to fit into one's pocket, yet which could be unfolded to a length of seven feet, showing a panoramic view of *The Congress of Nations*.

In mid-July a satirical sequence called *Donnybrook Fair; or, The Lancaster Races* was added. The publicity explained it as "twenty minutes of drollery and rollicking fun interspersed with comical situations, ludicrous scenes and life-like portraits." This appears to be a series of clown acts in keeping with the nature of the hippodromic program. Events included a grease pole competition, wheelbarrow, sack,

Mlle. Victoria, "Queen of the Lofty Wire"

and donkey races, and a sketch about the trading of horses, where "every character of enjoyment incident to the Irish nation is partaken of." There were burlesque fist fights and melees amidst the wildest confusion, as the women urged on their favorites.[14] Attached to this was a segment—the Lancaster Races—that included an English steeple chase.

Beginning Friday, June 26, and continuing to the following Friday, the regular performances were supplemented by amateur athletic contests, with prizes announced to be bestowed to the winners by none other than the titular proprietor, P. T. Barnum. Contestants were restricted to men who had never performed for hire or had never been compensated for teaching the feat in which they were said to excel.

Nixon had attempted something similar several years earlier. When his equestrian company neared the end of a run at Niblo's Garden in September, 1860, and attendance began to slack off, he included amateur gymnastic contests to the program. Calling it "The Gymnastic Tournament," he advertised that the management "was fully aware of the growing interest evinced by the community in regard to physical development and education among the amateurs by arranging a tournament, offering to individuals or societies ample opportunities for demonstrating the improvements made in healthy and invigorating exercises."[15] He followed this a week later with an announcement that professed of having many request from well-known citizens to continue the event. As a consequence, they were included for one week longer, "permitting any amateur of respectability to enter the lists, thus affording an opportunity for friendly emulation among the New York gymnasts; and allowing their fathers, mothers, sisters, and wives a fair chance to see their proficiency in active science."[16] These "exercises" consisted of four events with one presented each of four days—single trapeze, horizontal ladders, equestrian flights, and human pyramids.

The amateur contests at the Hippodrome commenced on Friday, June 26, and were shared daily between matinee and evening performances. "Whoever originated the idea of holding a series of athletic games at the mammoth place of amusement over which the Phoenix-like showman P. T. Barnum resides," wrote a *Clipper* correspondent, "evidently hit the nail square on the head, for thus far they have proved an undeniable success, putting money in the purses of those at the helm, and strengthening the foothold obtained by physical exercises in our midst." The competitions included pole vaulting, tossing the caber (a roughly trimmed tree trunk used in Scottish sports), standing long jump, *battoute* leaping, rope climbing, weight lifting, pole climbing, a bayonet exercise, shot put, wrestling, high jump, foot boxing, hop-skip-and-jump, dumb bells, walking, and various foot races.[17]

At the beginning of July it was announced that Barnum had arranged for twelve experimental balloon ascensions. For some time he had entertained an interest in navigational flight and more recently contemplated the launching of a transcontinental balloon from New York City, piloted by three aeronauts of different nationalities—American, English, and one from France or Germany; for which he was prepared to expend any sum necessary to accomplish. Money was to be no object.[18] He explained his intentions in a letter to the *Times*:[19]

> To the Editor of the New York *Times*:
>
> The subject of ballooning and its practical application to useful purposes has, as the public is aware, for some time past received my serious thought. I have discussed the matter with many scientific persons on this continent, and during my late visit to Europe I consulted with gentlemen who have made the subject a life-long study. When doctors disagree, who shall decide? I have found a diversity of opinion on every point involved; have had submitted to me almost every conceivable theory and all sorts of contrivances, some very ingenious and many more utterly impracticable. I'll try my own experiments, said I, and with this view have engaged Prof. Donaldson, a man of large experience, great perseverance, and undoubted courage, to make a series of experimental ascensions in a balloon manufactured expressly for the purpose. He will start from my "Hippodrome," in New York, twice a week, commencing, if possible, on the 7th inst., provided with the most improved instruments, and will furnish detailed reports of altitude, temperature, current, and course of the wind, &c.—every feature and particular that will interest science and the public. I hope by these ascensions to determine fully the question of the "easterly current," and decide whether it be a factor or a myth. Its existence being established, the voyage to Europe in such a balloon as I propose to build will be as easily and safely accomplished as a journey there in one of our best ocean steamers. Anxiously but confidently awaiting the result of these investigations, I remain the public's obedient servant,
>
> P. T. Barnum
>
> New York, Friday, July 3, 1874

Lighter than air navigation was an intriguing notion in the public mind. And there is no doubt that Barnum was serious about these experiments and fully intended to make a Barnum-like effort to conquer the problems of an Atlantic crossing. But it was also a shrewd move on his part to combine scientific study with show business rewards. As it turned out, Donaldson's lifts into space were remarkably instrumental in attracting audiences to the Hippodrome; and, indeed, became a feature nearly as important as the show itself.

Prof. Washington Harrison Donaldson (October 10, 1840-July 15, 1875) was born on Second Street, in the district of Southwark, Philadelphia. His father, David L. Donaldson, was for some years an Alderman for that part of the city. Young Donaldson was fond of sports, often practicing the art of walking a tight-rope and balancing himself on a ladder; he also became adept as a magician and ventriloquist. For some years he performed these feats in public, often preceding them by walking across the street on a rope stretched from the chimneys of two buildings. When he became interested in aeronautics, he constructed his own balloon and made ascensions from Reading, Allentown, and other Pennsylvania sites, at times performing on a trapeze hanging from the balloon's basket.

An interest in discovering the feasibility of crossing the Atlantic led to a working relationship with Barnum. A balloon of 30,000 feet capacity had already been constructed under the watchful eye of Prof. Donaldson, and another was being made. The ascensions were planned to occur twice a week for a period of six weeks.

The week of the July 6th was billed as "Derby Week." Announcements promised a culmination of all the numerous features— Kentucky runners vs. English thoroughbreds, pony flat races with "Lilliputian" jockeys, hurdle races by the leading ladies of the arena, standing and chariot races with Arabian horses. The daring charioteer, Mattie Lewis, was back from her injury and Mlle. Victoria, "Aerial Queen," was still pedaling her velocipede across the wire.

A series of walking matches between the letter carriers of the city, began on Monday, the 6th, and concluded on the following Saturday. The winners of the heats were E. McIntyre, Brooklyn; William H. Eagan, Station A; A. C. Primey, Station D; John H. Stark, Station C; Owen Lewis, Greenpoint; and W. Wild, Brooklyn. The final one-mile walk of the heat winners was scheduled on the night of July 13, during which McIntyre won in front of Eagan with a time of eight minutes and fifty seconds. For this accomplishment he received a diamond medal.[20]

On July 7, the day set for the first ascension, the balloon was carefully inflated during the matinee performance, presumably on the infield of the Hippodrome. But, alas, once filled, it was discovered there was insufficient lifting power to allow a proper ascent to be made. So the following day the Donaldson balloon was emptied and refilled with gas from another company, but not in time for the scheduled lift-off. Successful voyages occurred, however, on the following two days.

A major effort was made to bolster attendance for the final two weeks of the season. Prices were lowered, allowing all events to be witnessed for only 50¢. In addition, since professional pedestrianism was experiencing a decade of popularity at this time, it was announced that Edward Mullen, a well known pedestrian, would attempt to walk around the Hippodrome oval for a distance of 500 miles within a six-day period. For this the boxoffice would be open day and night, price 50¢.

Curiously, pedestrianism had become a spectator sport. Edward Payson Weston led the way with his many publicized endurance feats. He called attention to himself through a colorful sense of showmanship, always wearing a jockey costume with cap and boots and carrying a whip which he occasionally snapped to encourage his body to renewed efforts. Only a few months earlier, on May 10, he commenced a five hundred mile walk at the American Institute Hall at the invitation of several distinguished citizens.

Mullen's scheduled start was set at 12:05 a.m., July 20. An oval shaped track was positioned within the hippodrome course as an inner ring. This allowed for the walk to occur continually throughout the regular hippodromic program without interruption of any event. Representatives of the Committee of Arrangements were present at the site day and night to certify complete compliance with the rules of pedestrianism. Unfortunately, Mullen was forced to abandon the effort after the matinee on the 23rd because of swelling in one of his legs. He had sprained a tendon at an exhibition of his skills some two weeks earlier, from which, as he discovered, he had not fully recovered.

On Friday, July 24, Prof. Donaldson made what was advertised as a first "Grand Press Ascension" in the completed large balloon, *P. T. Barnum*, expressly constructed for experimental flight to ascertain the existence of an easterly current. The craft was made of the best materials and under the supervision of Donaldson himself. The gas bag supported a strong but light wicker basket, eight feet long, five feet wide, and four feet high, large enough to accommodate six or more people and provisions for two days of airborne adventure, still leaving space for ballast, scientific instruments, and other necessities.

The inflation began at 8:00 a.m. and the ascent occurred at 4:15, just five minutes following the finish of the matinee. Accompanied by five or six representatives of the local press, the Professor and his flying machine arose from the Hippodrome infield and disappeared through an opening in the canvas roof. A large crowd which had gathered outside the building greeted the passengers with cheers of approval. Donaldson, posing heroically, hat in hand, acknowledged the waving mass below.

The balloon drifted, not east, but rapidly northward and within a matter of fifteen minutes or so was out of sight. The length of flight measured about 400 miles in some twenty-five hours and finally came to an end at Greenfield, NY, nine miles from Saratoga, at 5:00 p.m. on Saturday. A second voyage for members of the press was scheduled for Tuesday, July 28. This practice of balloon excursions for newspaper people would, within a year, end in disaster.

The Hippodrome season closed on August 1. The only novelty for the week was another pedestrian event. C. N. Payne, "accepting Mr. Barnum's proffer for the free use of the walking course inside the inner enclosure of the Hippodrome," as the advertisement stated it,[21] appeared on Wednesday, July 29. At 9 o'clock that evening he commenced the feat of walking 115 miles in less than twenty-four hours. Starting off with his best time, he made the first mile in ten minutes and twenty seconds. But, in the end, he failed to meet his goal; for at 9:04 p.m. on Thursday, exactly twenty-four hours from his starting time, he had traversed only sixty-seven and a half miles.

Following the Saturday performance, the obstinate ostriches were rounded up, all the trappings and costumes were packed, and the whole of the arenic spectacle loaded up and conveyed to Boston, where Barnum's Great Roman Hippodrome opened under canvas just two days later.

All in all, *The Congress of Nations* proved to be the most luxurious show of pageantry ever attempted on this continent. The various races, with their thrills and spills and intense competitiveness, contributed continuous excitement throughout the entirety of the matinee and evening programs. The additional novelties during the run, particularly the athletic events, were inducements for repeat business and for bringing in a new segment of audience. The claim of performing to 20,000 people a day was not disturbingly far from the truth. Barnum's

LAST WEEK. LAST WEEK.
LAST WEEK
IN NEW YORK OF
P. T. BARNUM'S
GREAT ROMAN HIPPODROME.
The immense establishment will
POSITIVELY CLOSE SATURDAY, AUGUST 1,
and reopen in Boston, Monday, August 3.
ALL THE GREAT FEATURES OF THE SEASON,
reproduced for this, the
GALA WEEK AT THE HIPPODROME,
GALA WEEK AT THE HIPPODROME,
GALA WEEK AT THE HIPPODROME,
All the English Running Horses,
All the English Running Horses,
All the English Running Horses,
All the Daring Lady Riders,
All the Daring Lady Riders,
All the Daring Lady Riders.

CONGRESS OF NATIONS.
DONNYBROOK FAIR.
M'LLE VICTORIA.
THE GYMNASTIC ACTS.
LANCASHIRE RACES.
GRAND MENAGERIE.
Nothing omitted for the
LAST WEEK OF THE SEASON.
LAST WEEK OF THE SEASON.
LAST WEEK OF THE SEASON.
Doors open at 1:30 and 7. Performance at 2:30 and 8.

PROFESSOR W. H. DONALDSON,

The scientific aeronaut of the age, will make his SECOND GRAND PRESS ASCENSION from the Hippodrome TUESDAY AFTERNOON, July 28, immediately after the close of the brilliant races upon the GRAND COURSE. As this prolonged trip is to be undertaken purely in the interest of science, Professor Donaldson will be supplied with all the necessary instruments for ascertaining altitudes, currents, temperature, &c., and will be accompanied by several representatives of the New-York City Press. It is proposed to make this the longest aerial voyage UPON RECORD, and a full and detailed report will be published.

MR. C. N. PAYN, PEDESTRIAN, ACCEPTING MR. BARNUM'S PROFFER FOR THE FREE USE OF THE WALKING COURSE INSIDE THE INNER INCLOSURE OF THE HIPPODROME, WILL, AT 9 O'CLOCK WEDNESDAY EVENING, COMMENCE HIS GREAT FEAT OF WALKING 115 MILES IN 24 HOURS.

"crowning effort," at least for this engagement, had been a crowning success.

NOTES

[1] Loeffler, "A Re-Examination of the History of Madison Square Garden (etc.)," p. 8.
[2] New York *Times*, April 25, 1874; New York *Clipper*, May 2, 1874.
[3] Atlanta *Constitution*, February 23, 1891.
[4] New York *Times*, July 8, 1874.
[5] Lady riders included Alice Castineyra, Maud Oswald, Annie Yates, Mary Mason, Annie Davis, and Mary Walsh.
[6] Advertisement, New York *Times*, May 16, 1874.
[7] Barnum, *Struggles and Triumphs*, 1927 edition, p. 698.
[8] *Ibid.*, p. 697.
[9] C. H. White, "More Early Circus Memories," *Bandwagon*, December 15, 1944, p. 11. White was the son of Charles White, the boss animal man. As a youth, he rode in the elephant and camel races. His two sisters, Emma and Lizzie, rode in the horse races.
[10] New York *Clipper*, June 6, 1874.
[11] Advertisement, New York *Times*, May 26, 1874.
[12] Ella [or Helen] Grady, a native of Findlay, OH, was the former wife of G. G. Grady, proprietor of Grady's Old Fashioned American Circus.
[13] Richard J. Reynolds, III, tells us in a letter dated April 21, 1997, that he is quite certain it was a one horned Great Indian Rhinoceros *(Rhinoceros unicornis)*. But the business about the rhino's weight was pure hype. "The very biggest Indian rhinos on record have weighed only 4,000 to 4,500 pounds. The African black is about half that and the Sumatran not even a ton. White rhinos can go up to a whopping 6,000 to 8,000 pounds but there weren't any of them in captivity until after WW II." He went on to say: "Use of the adjective 'black' to describe the June 1874 Hippodrome rhino doesn't really help us. While, nowadays, that word has a very precise meaning, i.e., the two horned, African black rhino or *Diceros bicornis,* the word was used indiscriminately by 19th century showmen without regard to the true identity of a particular animal. I have seen it for rhinos that were either Indians or Sumatrans."
[14] *P. T. Barnum Advance Courier*, 1875. This edition, which is used as a source for this publication, is believed to be almost identical to the one issued in 1874.
[15] New York *Times*, August 28, 1860.
[16] New York *Times*, September 3, 1860.

[17] The contests were scheduled as follows: Friday, June 26—pole vaulting, rope climbing, mile race. Saturday, June 27—wheelbarrow race, tossing the caber, relief race, one-mile handicap race, standing long jump, one hundred yard dash, half-mile handicap. Monday, June 29—boy's race for under sixteen years of age, *battoute* leaping, rope climbing, half-mile walk, hand or health lift, half-mile run, pole climbing, bayonet exercise. Tuesday, June 30—100 yard race, shot put, three-legged race, 220 yards race, heavy hammer throw, wrestling, professional one mile walk. Wednesday, July 1—running high jump, wrestling, second trial, one-mile race, running long jump, hurdle race, 1/8 mile, eight hurdles three feet high. Thursday, July 2—quarter-mile race, *la savate*, foot boxing or a French style of self-defense, amateur one mile walk, hop-skip-and-jump, heavy single dumbbell, putting 100 pound dumbbell from shoulder, wrestling, final trial, hurdle race, 100 yards, four hurdles 3½ feet high. New York *Clipper*, July 4, 11, 1874.

[18] New York *Times*, September 18, 1873.

[19] New York *Times*, July 5, 1874.

[20] New York *Clipper*, July 25, 1874.

[21] New York *Times*, July 27, 1874.

VII
ROAD ENGAGEMENTS, BARNUM'S ROMAN HIPPODROME, 1874

The Connecticut Legislature issued a charter for the P. T. Barnum Universal Exposition Company, with a capital of a million dollars, on July 24, 1874. Barnum was recorded as president; W. C. Coup, as manager. Under the aegis of this enterprise the immense Roman Hippodrome, with its aggregate of some four to five hundred men, women, and children, four hundred horses, and an assortment of camels, elephants and other quadrupeds, went on tour to introduce its unparalleled marvels to audiences outside of New York City.

Barnum, in a letter to Samuel Clemens, wrote that he had an immense tent over 800 by 400 feet, which was transported to Boston, where seats were built to accommodate 11,000. There were over 1,200 men, women, & children engaged by him; 750 horses, including 300 blooded race horses and ponies; camels, elephants, buffaloes, English stags and stag hounds, ostriches, etc.[1] These numbers are pure "P.T." In the letter, Barnum was attempting persuade Clemens to mention the Hippodrome in any piece he might be writing for national circulation, which would explain an incentive to exaggerate.

According to another account, the main tent measured 450 by 250 feet, the dressing room tent was 190 by 140 feet, and there were others of various sizes for the menagerie, the stables, etc., requiring an open area of some ten acres. The hippodrome track was nearly one-fifth of a mile in circumference and about thirty feet wide. There were seats available for 10,000 spectators and room for another 5,000.

Probably because of the phenomenal success of the 1873 Barnum's Great Museum, Menagerie, Hippodrome and Traveling World's Fair, the "Hippodrome" in the title was being adopted by at least ten other organizations for this season.[2] This, however, did not seem to detract in any way from the prosperity of the Barnum show.

Nor were Prof. Donaldon's ballooning events unique to the Barnum aggregation. Balloon ascensions to lure audiences to the show grounds had in the last few years become a standard feature with several circuses. The first reference in the New York *Clipper* relating to daily, or almost daily, use of the balloon ascension as a free act was to George W. DeHaven's circus in 1870. Until evidence to the contrary appears, DeHaven has to be deemed the originator. He moved about in Iowa, Illinois and Indiana that season; then, at the end of July, R. E. J. Miles, a Cincinnati theatrical promoter, purchased the show, which continued to function under the DeHaven name. The company traveled the Ohio River on their boat *Victor* until they reached Wheeling, when they transferred to moving on the Baltimore and Ohio Railroad. At this time it was announced: "A balloon ascension is now made daily in connection with the circus."[3]

This type of free act caught on with other circus proprietors for the 1871 season. Agnes Lake's Hippo-Olympiad was mentioned in the *Clipper* early in January of that year; but she may have started the practice in late 1870. By that time, R. E. J. Miles had become managing director for Mrs. Lake, and George W. DeHaven was in advance of the show. The two men apparently carried their propensity for balloon ascensions with them; for at 1:00 p.m each day, or shortly before the start of Lake's matinee, Prof. J. W. Hayden fired up his equipment and went aloft. At least three other shows adopted the practice in 1871—G. G. Grady's Old Fashioned Circus, Wootten & Haight's Empire City Circus, and James Robinson's Circus. These shows used the hot air method for making the balloon ascend; whereas, Barnum's balloons were gas filled and, consequently, much safer, although more expensive to operate.

Taking the big Hippodrome show on the road was a gamble, in spite of the large returns of the preceding months. The recession that began in 1873 was still an impediment to circus operation. According to the *Clipper*, there were nine fewer major circuses leaving the barn that spring than in 1872. Then, by May, the Great Novelty Railroad Circus collapsed; in June, James L. Thayer's show and the Great Chicago organization were off the road. Older & Chandler disintegrated on August 15; and Noyes' Crescent City Circus followed at nearly the same time owing five months' salaries. The fall shows fared no better. By October, J. M. Hudson's company fell apart in Montreal; and the more reliable L. B. Lent circus closed in mid-November with people unpaid.

For the start of its 1874 road tour, the tents of Barnum's Roman Hippodrome were set up on the "back bay lands" of the Coliseum grounds, at the foot of Boylston Street, in Boston. The location was selected because of its large area of open ground and for its convenience to stops by the Beacon and Berkeley street cars of the Metropolitan Railroad. The three-week engagement began on the evening of August 3 and was successful from the start. Although the opening night house was not crowded; thereafter, the Hippodrome totaled over 20,000 patrons at the two performances each day and frequently turned people away.

On Friday evening of the 5th, Barnum made his first appearance. He responded to a general call from the audience by riding around the course in the barouche, bowing vigorously to his admirers. He was there again the following night. It should be explained that he did not travel with the show. His infrequent visits were the result of urging put forth by Coup and others to justify the Barnum name in the title. The people held a greater desire to see him than any oddity, animal, or performer on the bill.

What occurred at Boston in the way of performance and operational practice can exemplify what followed in the other four cities on the itinerary—Philadelphia, Baltimore, Pittsburgh, and Cincinnati. There were two shows daily, with the exception of opening day when there was no afternoon performance. With Sunday dark, the workmen had that day and most of the following Monday to make the move and set-up at the next stand. The doors opened at 1:30 and 7:00 p.m.; the performances began at 2:30 and 8:00. Admission for the orchestra chairs was $1.00; for the family circle, 50¢. Balloon ascensions were scheduled for Tuesdays and Fridays, weather permitting. Barnum's autobiography was still being sold; the advertisements claiming additions to the text up to March, 1874, with a total of 900 pages and a price "reduced" from $3.50 to $1.50. A free admission was still given with every purchase.

Traveling necessitated a few changes from the New York engagement. The show did not take the large collection of animals that had comprised the menagerie. Much of it was sent to the Central Park Zoo before leaving. Only ten cages went with the show, plus the hippopatmus, two giraffes, elephants, camels, and lions.[4]

The large cast of performers in *The Congress of Nations* did not go on the road either; rather, people were recruited at each stand. Advertisements were placed in the Boston papers for 900 supers to take part in the *grand entrée*. They were asked to apply on the morning of the 3rd, opening day.[5] This must have been quite a sight—lines of people of every size, shape, and manner, anxious to get into show business, waiting expectantly to be scrutinized by whoever was in charge, much

Rare View of the Hippodrome Tents
[Portion of a sketch, *Frank Leslie's Illustrated Newspaper*, November 7, 1874]

like a Hollywood open casting call. The job of selecting that many bodies that would fit into the available costumes and resemble the various ethnicities of *The Congress of Nations*, and within such a restriction of time, must have been colossal. "When the commander proceeds to the capture of Philadelphia," a correspondent suggested, "he will muster out these recruits, and enlist, in their places, Philadelphians."[6]

An advance crew of carpenters and other specialists preceded the show by several days in order to level the ground, prepare the hippodrome track and construct a tiered amphitheatre around it. The practice of erecting a wooden structure for seating at each stand in advance of arrival had been instigated by Barnum's circus managers to some degree the previous year.[7] One can only speculate that what with the rapidly increasing size of the Barnum canvas they felt the necessity to abandon the traditional means of bleacher construction, either/and fearing the sheer size of the configuaration would present a public danger from its instability and/or would be too combersome to carry from place to place—forcing the show to purchase lumber at each city and dispose of it there after moving on.

During this 1874 Boston stand, the *Daily Globe* revealed that before the Hippodrome company arrived the site had been the center of attention "for all the unemployed and unwashed of the city for many days." The completed work on the seating was given a favorable appraisal by the *Globe*:

> The construction is in the amphitheatre style, each row being sufficiently above the row in front to give every spectator a full view of whatever is going on in the arena. An examination of the framework beneath shows that ample precaution has been taken against a crash, and as a specimen of complete carpentry, wrought upon scientific principles, the work would commend itself to the artisan or the civil engineer.[8]

Barnum stated that it cost $50,000 to take the show to each place; so it comes as no surprise that a great deal of effort went into publicizing it. Newspaper advertising, generous in size and unrelenting in verbiage, was displayed well in advance of the opening. In Boston the first notices appeared on July 20, two weeks ahead of arrival. And, of course, the members of the press were offered trips aloft in the wickered receptical of the floating *P. T. Barnum*. Similar to the run in New York, the program on the road had novelties added on various days to induce repeat patronage. At each place arrangements were made for excursion trains to ferry people from the outlying areas to matinee performances—

particularly ladies and children—at a cost that included admission into the big tent.⁹ And for convenience, advance tickets were made available at downtown locations. In hopes of drawing from a wide perimeter, notices were presented through the press that Boston was the only city in New England that the Hippodrome would be visiting.

As would be his custom, press agent, D. S. Thomas, escorted the Boston newspaper representatives on a tour of the establishment. What they found were tents for cooking and serving food for 400 people, property rooms hung with costumes of the very best quality, etc. They were repeatedly impressed by the orderliness and systematic execution of everything, the "orderly chaos" that transpired. Despite the frantic changing of costumes, the rushing about of men and horses, every detail was planned and carried out with precision. One man was in charge of saddling and otherwise equipping the horses; another was responsible for readying the chariots; still another saw to it that the monkeys were tied in place, either for the Pompadeur drive or the steeple chase; and so it went with every facit necessary for the performance. In the supers' dressing area, no costume was delivered unless the performer's civilian clothes were left in its stead, which was exchanged when the costume was returned.

The people of the press were awed at the sight of the main pavilion. "To say that the interior of the tent is so many hundred feet long by so many broad gives a very slight idea of the size to unmathematical minds, but, when one thinks that Boylston Market building might be tucked away in one of the ends of it without seriously interfering with the sports of the race track, Boston people will get an idea of its size."¹⁰

The interior, as described in the *Daily Globe*, had an infield large enough "for two regiments to maneuver in without knowing of the presence of the other." The space was used for the gymnastic exercises, trapeze performances, wire walking, and various pageantries. The whole was enclosed by a fence to distinguish it from the oval race track. The track, one-fifth of a mile in circumference, was wide enough to allow a dozen racers to compete. In Boston at least, it was said to be as "well built" as any in the vicinity. This was separated from the orchestra chairs, which were presumedly on ground level, by a high board fence to protect the spectators from dust and danger of accident. A promenade, circling behind the $1 seats and raised some twenty inches above them, served as access to the rising platforms upon which the thousands of 50¢

spectators resided. But replacing the traditional bleacher-board seating were comfortable folding chairs—"Each Visitor Assigned to a Complete Independent Seat." For illumination, the five center poles were encircled with gas jets.[11]

Close by one of the entrances was an ordinary looking circus wagon which served as the hospital. The interior was lined with bottles and equipped with the essential instruments to dress the wounds and repair the bodily damages that surely occurred with frequency from the manic racing of man and horse.

The sideshow was operated by the Bunnell brothers. Their tent was larger than the ordinary sideshow top and the assemblage of curiosities more abundant. Zip, the "What Is It?" phenomenon, displayed his skill at "killing flies and looking pleasant"; there was the fat woman, reclining on a cushion; the fat boy, the bearded woman, and the Albino children. Around the tent were the cages containing the animals and birds.

The band was essentially the same as in New York. Led by Prof. Fritz Hartman, it was considered an artistically superior organization, sufficiently multitudinous for the music to fill the spacious canvas pavilion. Such familiar airs as "Hail Columbia," "The Marseillaise," "The Wearing of the Green," and "The Girl I Left Behind Me," gave full and cheery satisfaction.

The performance program was unchanged from that presented to New York audiences. On the occasion of the August 3 opening in Boston, at about the eight o'clock starting time the entry curtains, which allowed access from the assembly tent and dressing rooms, were opened and the barouche, used to convey the star performers into the arena, dashed in bearing the superintendent of amusement, Mr. James M. Nixon. It might be added here that the barouche was not merely a means of creating flamboyance for an entrance, although it did that effectively. The distance between the dressing rooms and the center of the hippodrome was so great that, not only would it tire the performers walking to and from the arena, but without rapid transit it would interfere with the intense pace of the total presentation; or, as it was phrased in the *Daily Globe*, "not a moment was allowed to pass without some attraction being before the eyes of the audience."[12]

As in the past, the program opened with *The Congress of Nations*, sometimes called *The March of the Monarchs* in the ads, the length of which occupied approximately thirty minutes. There followed in order: Satsuma and Little All Right, with their feats of balancing; the Roman standing race on two horses, featuring Stevens, North, and Hogle; monkeys' lapping around the oval in Mme. Pompadour's Carriage—"They look so solemn and wise as the ponies take them around the arena, one would think the bench of the Supreme Court were out for a ride on the Brighton Road";[13] a ladies race on thoroughbreds; Mlle. Victoria on the tight-rope; an English stag hunt; a two-horse chariot race with the Misses Saulsbury and Lewis; the liberty horse race; the English and American jockey race; the elephant and camel race; the race with monkeys mounted on ponies; Messrs. Loyal, Lazelle, and Millson on the trapeze; a four-horse Roman chariot race between Mme. D'Atalie and Mons. Arnaud; closing with twenty minutes of *The Lancaster Fair*—grease pole climbing, sack racing, donkey racing, wheel barrow racing, and a sequence of folk dances and native pastimes, all within an approximate two-hours to two-and-a-half hours running time.

As one might expect, the races were the outstanding attraction, shared only by *The Congress of Nations*. The other acts on the agenda were well received, but it was the men and women astride their mounts or jostled about in their chariots at top speed that supplied the wild excitement within the program. It was said that about half the male jockeys were English and the other half from this country. Of the upwards to fifty ladies connected with the show, five were the principal riders in the racing competitions—Mary Roberts, Maud Oswald, Annie Yates, Mary Walsh, and Alice Castineyra. The salaries for the riders ranged from $25 to $75 per week plus board. The thoroughbred race horses were not kept on the lot, but rather in stables in the vicinity of it. One reporter, in commenting on the size of the race course, found it to be quite satisfying. In comparing it to the ordinary circus ring, which he termed "unpleasantly suggestive of the meloncholy round which the clay-grinding horse of the brick-yard unceasingly travels," the Hippodrome oval was "broadened and extended to the proportions of a boulevard."[14]

It should be said that within these races there were frequent accidents. Sometimes the thoroughbreds were so severely injured as to require them to be put to death, creating a financial loss of from $900 to $1,900 each. Orders were sent to England almost every week for replacements so that the quality of the races would be maintained.

For Donaldson's ascensions, two sizes of ballons were used. One of them, holding 48,000 cubic feet of gas, could accommodate five passengers. The other, the *P. T. Barnum*, held 60,000 cubic feet and carried six to eight people without difficulty. A recurring problem was the inability of the local gas companies to fill the balloon's bag to capacity and to do it within a reasonable time. Weather was also an incumbrance to consistant take-offs.

The excitement generated from Donaldson's aerial events must have prompted the proprietors of a mercantile establishment, under the title of Oak Hall, to send up their own balloons as a means of promoting their place of business. According to a newspaper account, beginning at 10:00 a.m. on August 13, one of ten balloons was sent aloft every hour. Measuring about 100 inches in circumference and made of the best French rubber, they were manufacture by Brissonet & Cic of Paris. A streamer, eighteen inches long, was attached to each balloon, on one side of which advertised items placed on sale.

The second week of the run was bolstered through the announcement that the pedestrian, George F. Avery, would attempt to walk 500 miles in six consecutive days. He had accepted, it was written in the advertisements, "Mr. Barnum's proffer for the free use of the inner enclosure of the Hippodrome, and [would] commence his great feat at 12:05 a.m., Monday, August 10th."[15] Along with this was added the representation of an English stag hunt. The "plot" consisted of the assembling of the hunting party—some forty or fifty men and women—and then the hunt, as the hounds and hunters chased their quarry around the oval and eventually out of the arena. In no time a rider returned bearing the dead stag behind him on his horse. A *Globe* writer found it "as exciting almost as a hunt in real life, and the audience [was] liberal in noise to help the thing along."[16]

On Monday of the third and last week, a card from Barnum appeared in the newspapers, the meaning of which is perplexing:[17]

> Taking this opportunity to return my sincere thanks to the citizens of Boston and New England for their very liberal patronage, I beg to say that, notwithstanding a prevailing opinion that the Hippodrome will remain here longer than the period advertised, that it is quite impossible. All my arrangements are made in advance. Seats are already erected and advertisements leased for opening in Philadelphia on the 25th inst., and for returning two weeks afterwards to my Hippodrome building in New York. *Most positively*, therefore, the very last performance in Boston will be Saturday night next, 22nd inst. The public's obedient servant, P. T. Barnum
>
> Boston, August 15, 1874.

ATTENTION!

THIS STREAMER,

ATTACHED TO A TOY BALLOON (100 centimetres in circumference), was sent up from OAK HALL Boston, August —, 1874. Any one finding and returning it to the Proprietors, 32 to 38 North street, Boston, with full particulars when and where found, will be entitled to a reward of half a dollar.

(Signed) ————

The above is a facsimile of the printing upon each of the streamers attached to our OAK HALL BALLOONS

The STREAMERS are of WHITE TISSUE, 18 INCHES LONG, 4 inches wide in centre, narrowing to points at both ends. The Balloons are of Rubber, manufactured to our order by Brissonnett & Co., Paris and measure 100 centimetres in circumference.

BEGINNING THURSDAY, Aug. 13th, we shall despatch DAILY,

TEN BALLOONS EVERY HOUR,

From 10 A. M. to 4 P. M.

The reverse of the streamer bears simply an advertisement of such seasonable goods as we are now selling at reduced rates.

Full-sized Hammocks............................$2
Bathing Suits..............................$3 to $8
Bathing Shoes..................................50 cts
White Vests..................................$1 25

Should any of these Aerial Messengers fall into the hands of those to whom the slight reward offered is of no consequence, they will aid in an experiment, and confer a favor by promptly mailing, with particulars, to the

Proprietors of OAK HALL,
32 to 38 North St. Boston.

[Boston *Daily Globe*, August 14, 1874]

Back to New York after Philadelphia? Did Barnum want to discontinue the tour or was there no tour planned to begin with? The weather had not been ideal and perhaps the attendance was overstated. Or were the managers taking it one city at a time while the New York Hippodrome building was being refitted for the winter season? Then, too, there was a European tour being considered.

For the move to Philadelphia the whole show was loaded onto a steamboat, with the exception of the elephant, Bets. She was driven to Fall River by Charles White, the boss animal man. There, she was placed on the Fall River steamer for New York, then taken to New Jersey where White's horse and Bets were loaded onto a special car of the Pennsylvania Railroad bound for the Quaker City.[18]

A two week engagement began on Tuesday evening, August 25. The proprietors had encountered difficulty in finding a location for such massive spreads of canvas. An offer made for the Athletic Baseball Grounds was rejected. Finally, a spacious lot at the junction of Broad, Norris, and Diamond Streets was acquired. Long before the doors were to be opened the street was lined with carriages and the rush for tickets was immense by an opening night audience that numbered around 8,000.[19]

The first balloon ascension took place on Friday, the 28th. Six members of the Philadelphia press were conveyed aloft, crowded into the *P. T. Barnum* almost shoulder to shoulder. From the *Public Record* we learn that the lift-off occurred at 4:25 p.m. and within two minutes time the balloon reached a height of 4,200 feet, when two pigeons were released, followed by the drag rope (1¼ inch thick and 300 feet in length). Ten minutes from starting, the balloon reached an altitude of 5,000 feet, where the thermometer indicated a temperature of 72°. At 4:40 the height had been increased to 5,400 feet before the craft began a descent to a level of 275. At this point the drag rope was trailing through fields, displacing ears of corn and knocking over fences as it went. A small amount of ballast was thrown out to allow the rope to clear the obstacles below, but in no time the basket was scraping branches of trees in an alarming fashion. More ballast was extricated and by 6:05 a maximum height was reached at 6,500 feet before making a gradual descent.

The time came when it was apparent that some of the party had to be displaced. Lots drawn from a hat determined the order of debarkation. Mr. Janvier of *Forney's Press* was number one; Mr. Johnson of the

Inquirer, number two; Mr. Herbert of the *Age*, number three; Mr. Morgan of the *Public Record*, number four; Mr. Burke of the *Ledger*, number five; and Mr. Fisher of the *North American*, number six.

At 6:45 the balloon was landed on the farm of a Mr. Chandler of Centerville, New Castle County, Delaware. The men got out and the basket was loaded with stones to hold it firmly to the earth. They remained grounded until 8:10 when Donaldson gave the order to re-enter the craft. Voyagers number one, two and three, however, remained behind to cheer their more fortunate comrades as they were wafted away. At about 10:50 a landing was affected at Scottsville and the balloon was secured once more. The party then traveled about a mile to Parkesburg, where they spent the night. After breakfast they returned to the transport to find it incapable of lifting more than two people. It was determined that Morgan of the *Public Record* would accompany Donaldson for the remainder of the journey.

At 7:50 on Saturday morning the balloon was ready, sand bags refilled and stones removed from the basket. The two men boarded, paid their *adieux*, and floated northward, propelled by a gentle wind. It was Donaldson's intention to reach Baltimore. By 9:18 they had attained their highest altitude of 16,600 feet and were experiencing extremely cold temperature, a condition that determined a return to earth. At 10:10 the balloon landed at Nottingham Station on the Baltimore Central Railroad, in Chester County near the Maryland line. After a brief respite, up they went again, sailing around until noon, when they came to rest on the farm of a Mr. Edge. There they received the legendary farm hospitality, including a sumptuous dinner. By 5:00 p.m. the balloon was packed into the basket, loaded onto a wagon, and the high flyers were on their way to Havre de Grace, Maryland. There they caught the 9:00 p.m. train for Philadelphia, arriving at 11:30 and completing a balloon escapade that had lasted some thirty-one hours.[20]

Earlier in the week another Philadelphia aeronaut had met with a mishap. On August 25, Signor Pedanto, who had been making ascensions throughout the summer from a resort on Smith's Island, was to go up accompanied by Richard Smith, the proprietor's son, attired in the costume of a baboon. Four carrier pigeons were set to be liberated along the way. But the filling process did not go well, encumbered, as it was, by a high wind. At one point the balloon was buffeted against a tree, which resulted in piercing a small hole in the bag. Pedanto, determining the tear was of no consequence, went ahead with the scheduled ascension. But the balloon was only able to reach an elevation barely above the tops of buildings, for the gas was rapidly escaping. The moment of truth arrived when the craft ran into a flagstaff on the roof of the Pennsylvania Railroad building, at the corner of Fourth Street and Willings Alley, which caused it to collapse and drop to the street below. Miraculously, Pedanto was not injured in the one hundred-foot fall; his young companion, however, received two broken ribs and a bruised head. Quite typically, within ten minutes of the incident, a crowd of some 5,000 onlookers had gathered. And, oh yes, the pigeons, unharmed, were rescued by the police and returned to the aeronaut.

Donaldson's third ascension in Philadelphia was unique. As an inducement to bring people onto the Hippodrome lot, on the afternoon of Friday, September 4, the *P. T. Barnum* carried a party of seven ladies into the sky, an event claimed to be the first in the history of aerostation. Advance announcements revealed that the trip would consist of five members of the Hippodrome company—Alice Castineyra, Ella Grady, Maggie Taylor, Fanny Millson, and Mary Cotton—and two selected from the city.

The public response to the show was deemed so enthusiastic that the stay was extended for a third week. A September 3 advertisement heralding the additional performances included a message from Barnum himself:[21]

> Admonished by the thousands who nightly throng the streets and vacant grounds surrounding the Hippodrome—unable to gain admission—I have decided to prolong the Philadelphia season to, and including, Friday evening, September 11, positively closing upon that date. While all the brilliant races of the first week will be reproduced afternoon and evening, the vast programme will be increased at each exhibition by new and startling features, many of which are produced for the first time in America. Again advising ladies, children, and all who can do so to avoid the crowd by attending the afternoon exhibition—which equals in every respect that of the evening—I remain the Public's obedient servant,
>
> P. T. Barnum

In its recognition of the final week of performances, the *Public Record* proclaimed: "There has never been any popular amusement opened to the public that has drawn so largely as this great effort of Mr. Barnum."[22]

Baltimore was next on the itinerary. The tents were spread out on grounds adjacent to Madison and Boundary Avenues for the opening on Monday night, September 14. Contracts were made with the Baltimore and Ohio and the Baltimore and Potomac Railroads to accommodate excursioners. And to avoid the crowds on the lot, Baltimoreans could purchase tickets four days in advance at McCaffrey's Music Store, 205 Baltimore Street.

The man from the *American and Commercial Advertiser* was, like the others before him, overwhelmed by the performance. He found it "dazzling in its splendors, wonderful in its richness, bewildering in its variety, amazing in its vastness, startling in its scenes of skill and daring, exhilerating in the keen emulation of its contests, great, magnificent, stupenous."[23] He confirmed that the races were the great attraction, and particularly those in which the ladies were entered. "How they do ride! What keen competition they bring to their work! And what superb mastery of their fleet and restive animals they display!" he exclaimed. "No wonder that the vast audience bend forward and look with acutest sympathy for the varying chances of the contest as one or the other forges a little to the front, or shows some especial cleverness in maneuvering for a gain at the turns of the course!"[24]

The first of the series of balloon ascensions was set for Tuesday afternoon. But because the craft could not be inflated by the scheduled time, a notice informed readers that it was postponed until the 18th. To allow a prompt departure directly following the matinee and to insure that it would be ready on time, the gas company began the inflation process on the night before. This was not ideal because, after filling, as the balloon sat idle it lost some of its lightness by being adulterated with air which eventually disallowed the ascent to reach its full height.

Disaster struck on Sunday. A violent storm flattened the big top and dressing tent and ripped up the canvas. Over a dozen of the long quarter poles were broken, as well as a large number of folding chairs. A message was sent to New York immediately for fifteen or twenty sailmakers. The entire crew worked feverishly to make restoration. Before the Tuesday matinee, the huge tents were erect and ready for business. Only one day was lost. The unwelcomed weather condition disappeared, the sun came out and all was well again. The audience for the night show was judged to be as large, or larger, than any audience that had ever assembled in Baltimore.

It seems the second week was off to an even better start than the first. The man from the *American and Commercial Advertiser* saw promise of it excelling any week in New York, Boston, or Philadelphia.

"Not only is Baltimore turning out to the grand exhibition," he wrote, "but from the mountains of Alleghany to the sand hills of Worcester our country cousins are coming in by train and boat to swell the multitude that tends toward Barnumville."[25] An extra morning performance was given on the last four days, so great was the demand. Unlike circuses, the Hippodrome was being patronized by the best people of the city. "They see nothing wrong, nothing mean, nothing vulgar about its grand displays, its intense rivalries, its amusing exhibitions of animal nature, and probably a large majority of the professional and business men of this and other cities have gone to the great show and have lauded it as the grandest in the world."[26]

The last balloon ascension was scheduled for Friday, the 25th. Over fifty applications were made for the trip to the ethers, including some from the most prominent and wealthy people of the city. The final selection included E. P. Fulton, Jr. of the *American and Commercial Advertiser*, George Savage of the *Gazette*, James Hungerford of the *Sunday Telegram*, C. J. Fox of the Associated Press, and Miss Mary Irene Cook, daughter of W. I. Cook of the *Evening News*.[27]

After the Baltimore visit concluded following the matinee on Saturday, September 26, the show set up in Union Park, Allegheny City (now a part of Pittsburgh), Pennsylvania, opening on Tuesday night, September 29. The company was welcomed with unpleasant weather—light rain and cold; indeed, during their entire stay the thermometer held onto a daytime temperature in the 50° range. But the misbehaving of nature did not diminish the eulogizing given the performance in the Pittsburgh *Daily Gazette* of the following day: "The press had heralded its coming by flattering notices ... but no idea of the magnitude of the show could be gained from mere description, were it ever so brilliant and glowing—nothing but the evidences given to the senses by the eye could lead, even in a degree, to the true conception of its mammoth proportions, its splendor, or its diversity."[28]

Donaldson gave members of the press an aerial view of Pittsburgh and vicinity on Wednesday. At 1:00 p.m. the large balloon was placed near the north entrance of Union Park and the filling process begun. The work was delayed to some extent by a brisk wind that blew at intervals, causing small breaks that had to be repaired. It was 5:30 before the craft was ready for lift-off, and even then it had not sufficient gas to allow all of the passengers—which included representatives from the *Gazette*, the *Dispatch*, the *Post*, and the *Commercial*—to make the journey. After a casting of lots, the man from the *Post*, a Mr. Frank Higgins, lost out. The lucky voyagers, if one can call it lucky to be going up on a blustery day, ascended from Union Park at 6:25 p.m., journeyed about 120 miles, reached a maximum altitude of a little over a mile and a quarter, and finally came to rest ten miles from Latrobe at 10:15.

A challenge was made in the *Leader* of Sunday, October 4, which drew some attention:[29]

> I, J. C. Stroup, the proprietor of the Theatrical Headquarters and Club house, No. 84 Fifth Avenue, the acknowledged lightweight jockey of the United States, do challenge any one of P. T. Barnum's English or American jockeys to ride me a race for one mile dash, best two or three, to take place at P. T. Barnum's great Hippodrome on days hereafter mentioned.
> Yours Respectfully,
> J. C. Stroup

A reply to the challenge was forthcoming in the *Daily Gazette* of October 6:[30]

> Having ascertained that there is not the slightest doubt as to Mr. J. C. Stroup's respectability and social standing, and always ready to give the public all the amusement I possibly can, I accept the above challenge, conditioned as below, and with the distinct understanding that there shall be no betting. The race to consist of three half mile heats, best two out of three, and to take place on the Hippodrome track, the first heat on Friday evening, October 9, the second on Saturday afternoon, October 10, and the third on Saturday evening. Two English thoroughbred horses will be selected, and Mr. Stroup shall have the first choice. The horse he rejects will be mounted by one of our riders. To the winner I will present a beautiful gold-headed whip.
> P. T. Barnum

The challenger lost the first heat on that Friday evening, but there was no follow-up on the outcome of the other two in the *Gazette*. Whoever won was immaterial; the intended publicity for both parties was quite satisfactory.

The third balloon ascension, Tuesday, October 6, was for ladies only, called the second one of its kind ever made. As advertised, the female guests were to have a "picnic in the sky" and be returned to the city before darkness descended. They made the air journey in the company of Donaldson and press agent Thomas. Presumably, Thomas went

LAST WEEK! LAST WEEK!

BARNUM'S ROMAN HIPPODROME

UNION PARK, ALLEGHENY CITY,

AFTERNOON AND EVENING.

GALA WEEK!

Grand Culmination of all the Great Races this Week.

NO ACT OMITTED. All the Brilliant Features of the GREAT NEW YORK HIPPODROME reproduced for this Closing Week of the Great Sensation in Pittsburgh.

GRAND LADIES' PIC NIC
To the Clouds,
TUESDAY AFTERNOON, OCTOBER 6TH.

Upon this occasion PROF. DONALDSON will use for the first time in this city his New Mammoth Balloon, of a capacity of 60,000 feet. Prof. Donaldson will be accompanied by Eight Young Ladies, representing the fashionable circles of Pittsburgh and Allegheny City. The party will lunch in the clouds, and be landed in season to return to the city before night. The ascension will take place immediately upon the close of the regular performance upon the GRAND COURSE. No extra admission.

Doors open at 1:30 and 7. Procession moves promptly at 2:30 and 8 o'clock.

[Pittsburgh *Daily Gazette*, October 6, 1874]

along to toss out the sand bags, the fair passengers being too fragile for such manly occupation.

The final stand was in Old John Robinson's city, Cincinnati. The show opened at the Lincoln Park baseball grounds to adversely raw weather on Tuesday evening, October 13. Advance tickets had been sold at Church's Music Store, 66 Fourth Street.

The most memorable event of this engagement was the big balloon wedding—the "wedding above the clouds," the brainchild of the always alert press agent, D. S. Thomas. According to Kunzog, Prof. W. H. Donaldson and equestrienne Maggie Taylor had decided to join in matrimony. The prospective groom favored tying the knot a mile or so into the atmosphere, but his bride-to-be would have none of it. Thomas liked the idea for its publicity value and set out to find a willing couple. Charles S. Colton, of the ticket department, and Mary Walsh, a hurdle rider, had been thinking about a public wedding. Done. Thomas had his actors for the first ever aerial wedding and the biggest publicity event of the entire tour.[31]

On Saturday, October 18, the day advertised for the heavenly vows to occur, a crowd of nearly 50,000 outlookers gathered at Lincoln Park. The basket in which the ritual was to take place (having been displayed on the infield of the hippodrome track in anticipation of the ceremonial) was richly decorated with flowers and streamers—"The concentrating ring was wrapped in crimson; the supporting ropes of the carriage were white; the lookout was covered with snowy white muslin; the bottom of the basket was richly carpeted."[32]

As the filling of the balloon neared completion, the necessary supporting actors were assembled. The Rev. Mr. Jeffries was there from Pittsburgh to preside. Prof. Donaldson was gussied up in a new coat, morning pants, and boutonniere. Thomas was also there as Master of Ceremony—"bright in broadcloth and redolent of red roses." Donaldson's business manager, Harry Gilbert, having finished overseeing the inflating process, was about to signal the entrance of the pre-nuptials when—curses!—the balloon burst, splitting from top to bottom because of a defect in the netting.

To adjust to this embarrassment, Frank Whittaker announced to the Hippodrome audience that the wedding would take place on the following Monday. And to assuage disappointment, the bridal party was paraded around the track following the ensuing performance. The Hippodrome band entered playing Mendelssohn's "Wedding March," followed by two carriages. In the first was the bride and groom; in the second, the best man, general manager, W. C. Coup, and the bridesmaid, Annie Yates. Somewhere along the oval course the horse drawing the second vehicle balked, an indignity which forced the general manager and his escort to walk the remainder of the way.

The calamity of the occasion, following on the heels of the promoted expectations for it, was cause for public discontent. Was this just another Barnum hoax, pre-arranged to build an audience? It was "the topic at dinner tables, drawing rooms and barrooms that evening"; which prompted the company to be on the look-out to prevent violence or vandalism at the show grounds.[33] Too late for newspaper notices, hand bills were rapidly printed and distributed to announce the rescheduling.

Monday arrived along with Indian summer, an ideal day for a wedding on any elevation. The matinee crowd left the tent at about 4:30 to see, along with thousands of others, this unique event. The same supporting cast was there in all their finery. The balloon was in readiness, still frilled and flowered and filled with the necessary gas to propel the wedding party skyward. The Hippodrome band appeared from the tent, again playing the "Wedding March." The bridal retinue followed, the principal actors being the same as the previous Saturday. The entire cast of eight climbed into the basket, the signal for lift-off was given, the balloon rose from its site alongside P. T. Barnum's Great Roman Hippodrome, and sailed away into circus history.

Just a month earlier a marriage had occurred which made absolutely no ripples in the course of circus history, but which was indeed related to the narrative of the Great Roman Hippodrome. The man whose name it bore on every flier and every billboard and every newspaper advertisement took unto wife Miss Nancy Fish on September 16, who had just arrived on the *City of Montreal* the day before. The new and second Mrs. P. T. Barnum was forty years his junior. Unlike Tom Thumb's wedding to Lavinia Warren some eleven years earlier, the nuptials were held quietly before family and friends.

Throughout the season there had been injuries caused by the lady riders falling from their mounts. They were brave performers, perhaps too incautious in their eagerness to compete. On Friday afternoon of the 16th, Maggie Taylor was thrown by her horse when it missed one of the hurdles. She was assisted in remounting and, at her own urging, gamely finished the race; but once back at her dressing tent, she fainted.

Donaldson's Balloon Wedding
[*Frank Leslie's Illustrated Newspaper*, November 7, 1874]

At the night performance, Mary Mason was leading in the hurdle race until her horse lost its footing and pitched her forward onto the track. She was assisted off in a carriage.

Barnum and his wife were eminent visitor's for the final week of the season when the Great Roman Hippodrome closed a successful tour in Cincinnati. This Goliath of tented attractions had fared far better than its circus counterparts. Stowe's Great Western took an early departure in May; S. P. Stickney & Son, as well as G. G. Grady's, were gone by mid-summer; Wootten & Andrews were also dismembered in August; and Haight's Great Southern left the road that same month owing salaries. Following the Hippodrome's final performance on October 24, the weather being too cold to continue on to St. Louis and Chicago, the outfit was shipped back to New York City.

Throughout the tour there were only three names that recurred with frequency in the newpaper advertisements. P. T. Barnum's, of course, perhaps the greatest star of the nineteenth century in any form of entertainment, was always at the top of the display in large and bold type. Prof. Donaldson, Aeronaut Extraordinaire, was usually touted, but far from the top, and Mlle. Victoria, "Queen of the Wire," received occasional mention. The other performers went quietly about their work, accepting the laudatory newspaper reportage as their reward.

NOTES

[1] Barnum, *Selected Letters*, p. 189; written from Bridgeport, January 19, 1875.
[2] Warren & Henderson; Stevens & Begun; Haight & Co.'s Great Southern; Haight & Co.'s Great Eastern; Baird, Howell & Co.; Montgomery Queen; Howes' Great London; Burr Robbins; Harry Buckley; and VanHoughton.
[3] New York *Clipper*, September 3, 1870.
[4] White, August 15, 1944.
[5] Boston *Daily Globe*, August 4, 1874.
[6] *Ibid.*, August 14, 1874.
[7] Buffalo *Daily Courier*, July 2, 1873.
[8] Boston *Daily Globe*, August 7, 1874.
[9] The use of excursion trains was not original with the Barnum circus. An ad announcing them in connection with the Rivers & Derious show appeared as early as 1855 in the June 13 Richmond (VA) *Daily Dispatch*.
[10] Boston *Daily Globe*, August 4, 1874.
[11] *Ibid.*
[12] *Ibid.*

[13] *Ibid.*, August 10, 1874.
[14] *Ibid.*, August 6, 1874.
[15] *Ibid.*
[16] *Ibid.*, August 17, 1874.
[17] *Ibid.*
[18] White, *op. cit.*
[19] Philadelphia *Public Record*, August 26, 1874.
[20] *Ibid.*, August 31, 1874.
[21] *Ibid.*, advertisement, September 3, 1874.
[22] *Ibid.*, September 7, 1874.
[23] *Ibid.*, September 15, 1874.
[24] *Ibid.*, September 16, 1874.
[25] Baltimore *American and Commercial Advertiser*, September 22, 1874, p. 4.
[26] *Ibid.*, p. 4.
[27] *Ibid.*, September 25, 1874.
[28] Pittsburgh *Daily Gazette*, September 30, 1874.
[29] *Ibid.*, reprinted, October 6, 1874.
[30] *Ibid.*
[31] John C. Kunzog, "Barnum Show Balloon Wedding," pp. 11-12.
[32] Cincinnati *Enquirer*, October 18, 1874.
[33] Kunzog, *op. cit.*, p. 12.

VIII
WINTER SEASON, BARNUM'S ROMAN HIPPODROME, 1874-1875

The Great Roman Hippodrome came off the road after having attracted huge audiences in Boston, Philadelphia, Baltimore, Pittsburgh, and Cincinnati, and having astounded their citizens with its pageantry, novel racing competitions, balloon ascensions, and sheer immensity. But the season was marred by one pesky imitator—P. T. Barnum's New York Prototype Hippodrome, "presenting an exact counterpart to Barnum's Great New York Hippodrome." The *Clipper* reportage, however, did not use the Barnum name in connection with this show. There, it was variously referred to as "Buckley, Soulier & Co.'s Hippodrome," "Buckley's Hippodrome and World Race Congress," or simply "Buckley's Hippodrome." Nevertheless, the name of P. T. Barnum was prominent on some or all of the show's advertising.

The former Barnum employee, Harry Buckley, was the titular proprietor. Buckley (1829-1884) was born to the circus parents, Matthew and Marienne, and was brother of Edward and Page. By the time he was twelve years of age he was an accomplished rider and violinist. He was connected with various circuses before managing the concert privileges with P. T. Barnum's 1872 and 1873 circus.

The Buckley hippodrome show allegedly went out this year with three railroad trains, 800 men, women, children, and horses, 80 thoroughbred English fox and hurdle racers, a whole tribe of Iriquois Indians, 150 male and female champions of the Olympiad, $50,000 in Roman and Grecian chariots, $150,000 in domestic and imported thoroughbred race horses, $20,000 in racing elephants and camels, $20,000 in wardrobe, $150,000 in a free exhibit of living wild animals, and a daily expense of $3,000.[1] Such were the Barnum-like claims, much of which, Barnum-like, was an advertising exaggeration.

In a *Billboard* article, which related the career of George W. Hall, Jr., Hall, who was with the Buckley Hippodrome, stated:

> This show used nothing but fair grounds for lots. It consisted of all kinds of races—chariot, standing, , hurdle, etc., which all took place on the

SOMETHING ENTIRELY NEW!
FAC-SIMILE UNDER CANVAS OF
Barnum's Great Hippodrome,
UNDER THE MANAGEMENT OF
H. Buckley & Co.'s World Race Festival, Wambold's Royal English Menagerie,

SOULIER'S REAL ROMAN HIPPODROME &

UNIVERSAL FAIR
WILL OPEN IN CHICAGO
FOR ONE WEEK, COMMENCING
Monday, July 6,
ON LAKE PARK,

Foot of Washington-st., giving two entertainments the first day, viz: at 1 and 7 p. m., and three grand, full and complete exhibitions each subsequent day, at 10 a. m. and 1 and 7 p. m.

Admission to all only 50 cents; Children under 10 years, 25 cents.

Revival of all the classic sports and pastimes of the ancient Grecian and Roman Olympic Festivals and Games. Chariot Races, Roman Standing Races, Liberty Races, Elephant and Camel Races, Indian Races, Flat Races, Sack and Wheelbarrow Races, Walking Races by JAMES SMITH, the Champion Walkist of the world, who will walk against a running Elephant. Also, Steeple Chases and Hurdle Races by English Thoroughbreds, with all the Athletic and Gymnastic Sports of the Ancient Curriculum, such as Perilous Flying Men, Horculoan Cannon Ball Performers, Contortionists and Trapexists.

Strictly Moral and First-Class

The most intensely-interesting and attractive combination of Novel and Sensational Amusement Features ever known since the world began!

THE GREAT TRACK,
1,000 FEET AROUND,

Is COVERED BY A SPACIOUS CANOPY, and is flanked by Amphitheatre Seats capable of seating 10,000 people, with ample protection from sun and rain. The whole is brilliantly illuminated by night with 5,000 patent gas clusters and jets, presenting a grand and magnificent sight. To avoid the great crowds of the evening, the morning and afternoon exhibitions are more preferable for families, ladies and children.

Will exhibit in Watertown July 30; Oshkosh, 30; Green Bay, July 1; Appleton, 2; Fond du Lac, 3; Milwaukee, 4.

H. BUCKLEY & CO.,
Proprietors.

SCOUNDRELISM.

I am informed that parties are using my name in the West, advertising their shows as "reproductions of

P. T. BARNUM'S ROMAN HIPPODROME,"

also using the name
"**BARNUM**,"
and sometimes
"**BARNUM & CO.**"

Whenever these, or any other devices, are resorted to by showmen to induce the public to think I have any interest in their shows, unless I am plainly announced as the MANAGER, and my PORTRAIT published in newspapers and placards, I denounce such showmen as scoundrels, impostors and swindlers, and I will prosecute them for using my "trade-mark" to deceive the public. The ONLY shows which I have at present are my GREAT ROMAN HIPPODROME, removed temporarily to Baltimore, and, perhaps, to Pittsburgh and Cincinnati, and to return to my great Hippodrome building in New York very soon; also my traveling MUSEUM, MENAGERIE, CIRCUS, AND WORLD'S FAIR, at present in the State of New York.

Let the public BEWARE of men who, having inferior shows, attempt to palm them off as mine.

The Public's obedient servant,

P. T. BARNUM.

Bridgeport, Ct., Sept. 9, 1874.   25-1t

---

race track. They had circus acts of all kinds which were shown in front of the grand stands.[2]

At least at the outset of the season, the Buckley aggregation set up on fair grounds with no canvas covering, which allowed only daytime performances. But the *Clipper* announced in June that a tent was acquired, the size of which gave dubious boast to "a quarter-mile track, half mile canvas" and accommodations for 10,000 people.

If the *Clipper* was correct about a tent being used, the race course was only about an eighth of a mile, three times around being the length of the contests. The bills advertised an illumination of "five thousand patent cluster gas jets," "The Grandest World Race Congress

Ever Known," "Magnificent Chariot World-Race Festival," a game of La Crosse by Black Hawk's tribe of Iroquois Indians, lariat throwing, a walking match, marksmanship, the ferocious Marquesas Cannibals, sack races, foot races by Indians, a $30,000 talking machine, and "Three Splendid Bands of Music." Pictorials in the ads implied elephants, camels, ostriches, Indian encampments, and an iron-jaw lady. The list of managerial positions included W. Van Houghton, general manger; E. C. Buckley, first assistant; H. Buckley, secretary; Mons. Soulier, race master; W. C. Crum, advertising agent; and Yankee Robinson, general superintendent. Others listed on the bills were Mlle. Waldon, queen charioteer; Black Eagle, Captain of La Crosse; Prof. Max Upp, aeronaut; Sargeant Standish, cannonier; and James Smith, champion walker. Admission 50¢, children half-price.

The show was routed through the Midwest—Minnesota, Illinois, Indiana, and Michigan. There is no appearance of a collision with Barnum's Roman Hippodrome, but the *Clipper* reported in June of a set-to with the Adam Forepaugh circus. Warring through Illinois, "much bad language and dirty linen was given to the public," with the Forepaugh outfit winning the battle of words. The over-sized outfit went into bankruptcy before a full season was completed.

Up to this point, as it moved back into New York City, the genuine Barnum's Roman Hippodrome had enjoyed both critical and financial success. But agent John Dingess, in his unpublished manuscript, has related a disagreement between W. C. Coup and P. T. Barnum which, if true, brings incite to the change in prospects of the organization from this point in our narrative.

He stated that in the spring of 1874 Coup's health gave out and, for rest and recovery, he went to Europe. This must have been directly following the first New York season; for, thereafter, we find no mention of his name in the newspaper commentaries until the final stand in Cincinnati. Making his headquarters at Baden-Baden, Dingess states, Coup spent the summer in travel. Some time during the trip he arranged to bring out a piece called *Joan of Arc* for the New York winter season. He ordered the construction of five hundred suits of silver armor from a Birmingham, England, establishment; and in Spain he contracted a celebrated Barcelona ballet master named Espenoza. After arrangements were completed, he received a cable from Barnum to cancel all contracts and come home. Coup insisted on developing a new attraction for the winter Hippodrome program, feeling that it would be disastrous to open with "the same old traps and *Congress of Nations* and wardrobe that had been used since the spring before." This started an angry dispute by cable, "which cost them several hundred dollars."[3] Coup arrived back in the United States still asserting that they would end up losing money for the want of new attractions. As it happened, he was right.

The Hippodrome re-opened on November 2. Following the company's departure in August, the building was altered for winter performances. A new roof of iron and glass replaced the canvas one. The interior was redecorated, new matting laid on the concrete flooring, the railing around the interior arena was lowered, and rows of gas lights were added. In the auditorium, the cane-seated chairs and private boxes on the Madison Avenue end were removed and replaced with benches, making the seating space at either end of the building available for the 50¢ admissions. Iron folding chairs, upholstered in red enameled cloth were placed on the 26th Street side, which, along with the seats on the opposite side, were scaled at $1. The track and arena were put in better condition than they had been in the spring. The surface of the former was leveled so as to prevent occurrence of accidents and covered with softer and better soil. The hallways and stables were improved and heated by hot air furnaces. New outfits and trappings were purchased for men and beasts. As an incentive to draw the youngsters, a 25¢ admission for children under ten years of age was offered on and after November 30. Otherwise the place and program were much the same as when the show departed.

A new spectacle, *The Fete at Pekin*, was introduced on November 23, replacing *The Congress of Nations* entrée. The reader may recall that Nixon had used this theme in 1860 at Niblo's Garden. For this new event, the interior of the Hippodrome was profusely decorated with numerous and colorful flags. The grand procession included the appearance of the 1690 Chinese Emperor, Haamti, seated in a palanquin borne by a number of Mandarins and followed by a cavalry of Tartars. Ladies of the Emperor's court were also transported on litters. Accompanying these dignitaries, there were lantern and fan bearers, servants beating gongs, a winged dragon guarded by citizen soldiery and Mandarins bearing spears. After circling the track, the Emperor and his court took seats upon a platform, while the cavalry and foot soldiers performed a number of evolutions; followed by a Chinese ballet under the direction of Prof. George W. Smith, with the dancers led by Carrie Seymour and

Chariot and Liberty Races [Barnum's *Advance Courier*, 1875]

Mattie Lewis. Next, the Jackley Family of acrobats performed a pyramid act on a series of raised platforms placed at equal distances about the interior; and the Kennebel Brothers cavorted as Chinese clowns.[4] Satsuma and Little All Right exhibited feats of equilibrium, followed by Yamadiva, the contortionist. The spectacle concluded with Ling Look and his fire-eating act while mounted on the top of a car drawn by a number of horses. As the procession came to an end, a display of fireworks erupted from the car, leaving Ling Look standing amid the glittering inferno.[5]

An unexpected gladiatorial event, but as ferocious as its Roman antecedents, occurred on December 4 when two rhinoceroses in the Hippodrome menagerie faced off in what was termed the "battle of the beasts." At about ten o'clock that morning, for some inexplicable reason, Charles White put the two animals, a male and a female, in the same pen. Within minutes a roaring was heard, the like of which promptly cleared the building of sightseers, who fled through any egress available to them. The racket of the rhinos, like a contagion, spread throughout the great edifice, taken up by all the creatures of the wild—elephants, lions, tigers, panthers, hyenas, and even the birds, as they joined in a deafening chorus of disharmony.

Assistant manager, Charles Fuller, and some reluctant employees rushed to the scene of trouble, along with White and Dan Castello. They were unable to communicate verbally, so tumultuous was the uproar, while all the time they expected total pandemonium to break loose amongst the caged and fettered menagerie collection. Meanwhile, the keeper of the male rhino, a lad called "Alligator," jumped into the fray in a daring attempt to dissuade his charge from such ungentlemanly conduct. But the female was bent on destruction and would not be pacified. After some point, while the two combatants were squared off for another charge at each other, the men managed to throw a sizable collection of lumber between them. This maneuver created a separating fence which effectively brought an end to the fury. The gladiators received only minor abrasions and Alligator escaped unharmed. The disruptive female rhino, the actual aggressor, who had just joined the menagerie, was with some difficulty placed in the wheeled cage in which she had arrived and taken to the far end of the building. And calm was restored.[6]

One cannot be certain what caused the fracas. We are told by Richard J. Reynolds III, a zoological authority, that courtship among

SACK RACE

Indian rhinos is a notoriously savage affair. The female, unbeknownst to the handlers, could have been in a mating condition. Certainly the two were unfamiliar. The confined quarters within the Hippodrome gave neither a means of escape. Possibly, combat the only option.

There is no certainty as to the identification of the beasts. But most propably, one was the so-called "black" rhino that had been placed at New York Central Park Zoo while the Hippodrome company was on the road. The other, perhaps the male, was circus proprietor John O'Brien's animal sent up from Philadelphia for the winter engagement.

Barnum's press people were trying everything they could concoct to bring the audiences out. In a mid-December advertisement, announcing the final week of the Jackley Family, a new system of heating was featured which had "proved one of the most valuable of modern inventions, and supplie[d] a want long felt in the amusement buildings of New York." No dangerous draughts and oppressive heat, the claim read, but a perfect, even temperature throughout the building.[7]

The pantomime of *Bluebeard* was announced for the Christmas season beginning December 23, having been postponed from the 21st. For the production a large excavation was made in the center of the arena and covered with a platform which contain a series of traps. A subterranean passage connected this with the dressing rooms on the Fourth Avenue side of the building. By the use of machinery below, Bluebeard's castle and other scenic devices were made to rise and sink as occasion required. A large, movable platform, made in sections, was used for the ballet dancing. And paraphernalia for the various pantomime tricks were stationed along the sides of the arena and rapidly placed into position by a corps of workmen.[8]

The extravagant pantomime included the portrayal of a Moorish village with a Turkish ballet in progress, a grand procession featuring the Great Pashaw, Bluebeard mounted upon an elephant, etc. Bluebeard's castle arose from the ground in full view of the spectators, followed by a grand ballet. A chamber appeared, within which were exhibited the headless wives of Bluebeard; there was the arrival of Selim and his friends to rescue Fatima and Irene; there was the usual transformation of Bluebeard into Clown, Selim into Harlequine, etc. At one point the Clown was shot from a mammoth cannon—ingredients of a traditional Christmas pantomime. Following this, the races were given.

Competition for the Hippodrome at this time was L. B. Lent's New York Circus, which had opened in the city on Tuesday evening, December 22. The Terrace Garden Theatre was converted for arenic performances with a ring constructed on the floor of the parquet directly in front of the existing stage. The company included such well-known figures as Frank and James Melville, Henry Welby Cooke, Tom Watson, and William Conrad. But business proved to be light. The location of the theatre was unfavorable for winter attendance and the Hippodrome was siphoning off some of the circus audience.

In a continuing attempt to encourage more attendance, the Hippodrome management made a number of adjustments following the holidays. Admission prices were reduced to 30¢ for the family circle, 50¢ for orchestra chairs, $1 for reserved seats opposite the grand stand, and half price for children in each section. This change increased the low priced attendance but slowed the purchase of the more expensive seats. In a December 29 advertisement, it was announced that, "as a feature of special interest to the thousands visiting the menagerie," immediately following the matinees the animals would be fed. *Bluebeard* and *The Fete at Pekin* were withdrawn and the ballet corps dispensed with after January 2. Only the various races, *Indian Life on the Prairie*, and *At Donnybrook Fair* remained.

Beginning with January 14, trotting races for a purse were introduced—the purses ranging from $25 to $300—which tended to revive attendance somewhat. The track, covered a couple of inches deep with sawdust or tan bark, required seven laps to make a mile. Although suitable for indoor competition, these conditions were unfavorable for creating the fast times of the normal outdoor race course.

At the beginning of February a tournament scene was added, consisting of armored knights, representing various states of the Union, who, riding a full speed, attempted to spear with their lances ivory rings, some three inches in diameter, which were suspended from the ceiling over the hippodrome track—one on the northerly and the other on the southerly side of the course. The victor was crowned by a lady symbolizing the Queen of Beauty. Was this inserted to make use of the five hundred suits of armor Coup had purchased in Birmingham?

On February 15 a final novelty was presented, called *Salesday at Tattersall, or, Scenes Among the English Turfmen*. The pageant re-enacted a horse auction, showing how buyers were taken in by sharpers, all amid a background of street singers who warbled appropriate ballads. This sequence was followed by a burlesque race between two broken down steeds, terminating with police arresting the jockeys for cruelty to animals. The trotting matches continued until the Hippodrome closed on February 27. The season over, the employees were given a reunion at Ferrero's Assembly Rooms, Tammany Hall, on the evening of March 8.

Nixon took a benefit at the Hippodrome on March 22. Through Barnum's generosity he was given free use of the building for the occasion. "Mr. Nixon's well-known popularity and long career in the equestrian profession as performer and manager," a writer remarked, "will doubtless insure a large attendance, and enable him to put before the public a strong array of volunteer talent."[9]

The Hippodrome reopened on March 29. The program at this time included a scene from *Bluebeard—A Vision of the Houris*, consisting of an Amazonian march by a group of ladies attired in new armor of gold and silver leather. There followed feats of balancing by Satsuma and Little All Right; a flat race between five female riders; the monkey and carriage routine; a two-horse chariot race; a Shetland pony race; a Roman standing race by Stevens, Hogle, and North; Mme. D'Atalie's cannon ball act; *Indian Life on the Prairie*, with new costumes; a race between English and American jockeys; a race between monkeys on ponies; a female hurdle race; a four-horse chariot race; gymnastics by Lazelle & Millson; and the whole closing with *The Fete at Pekin*, with new costumes, trappings, etc.[10]

For the week of April 5 *The Congress of Nations* was re-introduced, with new costumes and harnesses and with chariots re-gilded. Trotting races were also brought back. Performances were given for only the week, after which the doors were closed for the indoor season on April 10. This two-week reopening of the Hippodrome was merely a means of preparing for the road, a slimming down and stream-lining of the original program to make it transportable for the up-coming summer tour.

The season had not drawn well enough to be profitable. By this time the nation was in the throes of hard times caused by a general business and financial deflation. The panic in 1873, the most severe the country had experienced, was affecting the lives of both country and city dwellers through lowered incomes and unemployment. Added to this, no new attraction had been devised to kindle the desire of many New Yorkers to revisit the Hippodrome. The lowered price scale was successful in increasing attendance, but lowered prices do not pay for large overheads. Coup's prophesy turned out to be correct.

The final program bill announced the Hippodrome lumber was to be sold at auction on Friday morning, May 28, about 150,000 feet of it. Presumably this was what had been used for the tiered seating. The six 60-foot spars which had supported the canvas cover were also sold, along with 3,000 chairs.

With the departure of the Great Roman Hippodrome for good and all, the former New York and Harlem Railroad Co. building took on a more sedate aspect under the proprietorship of P. S. Gilmore. The place was transformed into a summer garden with broad, gravel walks, blooming flowers and assorted greenery, wherein visitors could delight in refreshments and listen to Gilmore's one hundred piece orchestra. Subsequently, it was used for various events—pedestrian contests, a skating rink, circus exhibitions, more concerts—until 1879, when it became known as Madison Square Garden.

NOTES

[1] Newspaper advertisement for the appearance in Appleton, Wisconsin, July 2.

[2] *Billboard*, June 24, 1922.

[3] Dingess manuscript, pp. 372-373.

[4] Nathan Jackley, an Austrian acrobat, came to the United States in 1874 after starring with the Rosinski Troupe from Russia. Shortly before joining the Barnum organization, he had Jackley's Vienna Circus in Cincinnati. He is remembered as being the originator of an act called the "Jackley Drops." It consisted of tables piled eight high, with a ninth placed next to them. Standing on the eighth, Jackley dropped backward and landed on his hands on the floor level ninth; then did a backward leap, which landed him on ground level facing the tables. The Kennebels—François, Joseph, and Eugene, French clowns and pantomimists—came to America with Howes Great London Circus in 1864. Joseph was unique in that he performed without speaking, a comic device heretofore not used in the American arenas. The boys' sister was the famous equestrienne, Madame Dockrill.

[5] New York *Clipper*, December 5, 1874. Ling Look had performed at James M. Nixon's Chicago Amphitheatre in 1872.

[6] Clipping from *The Era*, December 27, 1874, from the circus collection of the Milner Library, Illinois State University, contributed by R. J. Reynolds III.

[7] New York *Times*, December 16, 1874.

[8] New York *Clipper*, January 2, 1875.

[9] New York *Clipper*, March 20, 1875.

[10] New York *Clipper*, April 3, 10, 1875.

IX
FINAL TOUR, BARNUM'S ROMAN HIPPODROME, 1875

In spite of the disappointing winter season, the Barnum establishment set out for a daring summer tour. The intent was to route the Hippodrome in the manner of circuses, covering more cities throughout the East and Midwest, and remaining for shorter periods of time than in 1874. Although there were extended stays in places like Philadelphia, Brooklyn, Boston, Chicago, St. Louis, and Cincinnati, for the most part the itinerary was made up of one-day stands. This was a huge undertaking for an outfit so large and so cumbersome, one that had never before been attempted.

Barnum was well aware of the gamble he was facing. In a letter to Samuel Clemens, he wrote, "I can easily lose half a million of dollars next summer unless I can in advance so awaken and electrify the country as to have everybody join in getting up excursion trains so as to hit me where I open the hippodrome." If he could accomplish this, he continued, "I can make half a million, so it is a pretty big stake to play for, hence my anxiety."[1]

How was such an undertaking managed? Two tents, approximately 500 by 300 feet were used for the hippodrome performance, one of which was already set up at the next stand by an advance crew. There were also carpenters and workmen ahead to prepare the ground and build the tiered seating levels. A show advertisement in a Janesville, Wisconsin, newspaper boasted that the wooden amphitheatre provided room for 15,000 spectators and cost from $1,000 to $3,000 to erect at each stand. On leaving a town the lumber was sold. An item in a Lowell, Massachusetts, paper announced the auctioning of approximately 50,000 feet of it. We learn from the Dubuque *Herald* that "fifteen men and a small lumber yard" were at work in that city four days before the show arrived.:[2]

> NOTICE.—The many thousand feet of lumber, from which the amphitheatre is erected in every stand, will be offered for sale at public auction on the Hippodrome grounds the day after the exhibition. The

lumber is valuable for building and other purposes, in most cases answering as well as new.

A portion of this went to the Home of the Friendless and the balance was sold as booth building material for the forthcoming fall exposition.

Beside the main tent, there were five others for the 300 to 350 horses, a "hotel" where 300 or more men were fed, dressing rooms, and an outer area, the size of the usual circus big top, where the performers formed into line. There were also facilities for the blacksmiths, the harness makers, and the tailors. The problem of transporting a show of such immensity by rail was solved by constructing cars twice the usual size and designed for a specific purpose. Cars, for example, were built with stalls commodious enough to allow the stock horses to lie down and rest while making the move. And the efficiency by which the whole was transported and erected would put many modern organizations to shame. The entire outfit could be unloaded from the rail cars within a matter of thirty minutes and be completely assembled for performance within some six hours.[3]

A description of the entire aggregation leaving their winter home in the Hippodrome building and embarking on special trains to Philadelphia was set down in the New York *Sun* of April 12. At 1:00 a.m. on Sunday morning of the 11th, following the evening performance, the entire show began its procession to the ferry which was to take it to the Jersey side. Some one hundred trained horses led the way with a rider for every four. They were followed by two elephants and a long line of camels. Then came the closed cages and the baggage wagons. It was Hurd who gave the word for the procession to start down Fourth Avenue, filling four blocks in its entirety. Through Astor Place to Broadway, down Broadway to Courtlandt Street, they rolled, and thence to the river crossing.

At the ferry, after a delay caused by an insufficient number of boats to handle the large show, the stock and wagons were taken across to Jersey City where three trains with twenty-five cars each were waiting. Before daylight the long caravan of wagons and beasts were safely loaded for the short trip to Philadelphia. Then the hundreds of performers and associates were packed into twenty passenger cars. And at 7:00 a.m. the trains pulled away. The Great Roman Hippodrome had hit the road.

The advertising was extensive. Three and four column newspaper ads were not unusual. Within them Barnum issued a broad challenge to his competitors. If it was accepted and proven to the contrary, he would give $5,000 to charities for each of the following claims: that the Barnum Exposition Company imported more thoroughbred horses than all the combined shows in America—that it expended more money for the erection of wooden amphitheatres than the daily expense of any traveling show—that it had more musicians than any two traveling shows—more performers than any five shows combined—and on through the list of all the features of the Roman Hippodome.

We learned from him as early as April that certain impostors in Cincinnati had copied his bills, posters, cuts, and advertisements in an attempt to pass as the authentic Hippodrome exhibition. At that time he cautioned the public against the deception. The Cincinnati *Daily Enquirer* suggested that the pretended Hippodrome was the "wreck of that stupendous fraud known as the Great Eastern and Great Southern Circus and Menagerie combination, which exploded at Selma, Ala., the 16th of last November, a number of horses having to be sold to pay the expenses of shipping the show to this city, where the proprietors left a number of their employees unpaid and penniless, and vamosed."[4]

These "impostors" of Barnum's paranoia were proprietors of an organization called "America's Racing Association," which opened at the Union Ball Grounds in Cincinnati for a week on April 5. The culprits were George W. DeHaven, general manager; R. E. J. Miles, treasurer; and Andrew Haight, director. The hippodrome exercises were supervised by none other than Dan Rice. Sam H. Joseph was the general agent; and John Evans, the contracting agent.

The advance notice in the *Clipper* stated that there were two billing brigades with six persons each; and, in all, there were twenty-two people in the advance. The show personnel numbered over 300, which included forty lady riders and three lady gymnasts, twenty-five acrobats and gymnasts, twelve leapers, and fifteen "specialty artists." There were thirty-six cages of animals, three performing dens, four elephants, six camels, and four buffaloes; over three hundred horses and fifty ponies; over two hundred sets of new harness and twenty ladies' saddles; elaborate wardrobe under the supervision of R. E. J. Miles, which consisted of over three hundred pieces of armor and dresses representing the different nationalities. The six center pole tent accommodated seating for 12,000 people, 1,000 of which were reserved chairs, and all surrounding a track of over 1,100 feet in circumference. The procession was comprised of two bandwagons, twenty-two musicians, one steam calliope, twenty Persian and Roman chariots, six chariots representing the leading nations of the world, two tableau cars, and two pony chariots. The company traveled by rail, employing seventy cars, which included two Pullman sleeping coaches. The original investment was said to be around $500,000.[5] We emphasize that the above are details submitted to the *Clipper* by the management, not necessarily a factual account of the company's size and worth.

The program was quite like the Barnum-Coup-Castello-Nixon model. The tent was comparable and the program followed somewhat the format of its predecessor. There was an opening not surprisingly called *The Congress of Nations*, which was followed by races of every description. Public trotting and running races occurred daily with two $100 purses and a silver goblet for the horse making the best time. The menagerie was also an important feature.

After taking to the road, the show encountered bad weather. In Indianapolis on the 17th, an acrimonious wind prevented the tent from being raised for the matinee, but by late afternoon the canvas was up and ready for the evening performance. Then, at about 7:00 p.m., although the wind began a return, the doors were opened to an audience anxious to see what the America's Racing Association was about. Following *The Congress of Nations* procession, the storm reached a gale intensity, forcing a warning that, although it was dangerous, the show would continue. The audience remained until the tent poles began to dance, an entertainment not included in the price of admission. At this point, the management discontinued the program, emptied the place of patrons, and lowered the canvas.[6] A St. Louis stand began on the 19th to more stormy weather, although business improved as the week continued.

The show was in Chicago at Lake Park for a week beginning April 26. Of the street parade, one observer commented: "There are many novelties but we failed to see the gorgeous golden chariots, tableau cars and rich trappings which were so strongly advertised, while, on the contrary, everything was comparatively neat and substantial, but far from being gorgeous." He found the only "first-class features" within the performance to be the four-horse chariot races and the quality of the racing stock.[7] On the other hand, an Auburn, New York, correspondent saw the street parade as a "gorgeous affair" which attracted much

Herkimer, June 1, 1875.

DEAR SIR:—The enclosed Complimentary Ticket will admit you to the GREAT AMERICAN HIPPODROME, MENAGERIE AND CONGRESS OF NATIONS, which will exhibit in

HERKIMER, ON FRIDAY, JUNE 4TH,
AFTERNOON AND EVENING.

We have the largest Canvas in the World, the greatest number of Performers and Thoroughbred Horses, the largest and best Menagerie, and the most enjoyable entertainment ever offered to the public. Our Grand Street Procession, led by DAN. RICE, Director of Amusements, will be made between 10 and 12 o'clock in the morning, and is of itself better worth seeing than the entire performance of half the traveling shows. Our Immense Exhibition has excited the envy of certain itinerant showmen, who are resorting to unfair means to induce people to believe that our show is not coming. We shall positively exhibit on the day announced. Your influence with your neighbors is respectfully solicited.

Very truly yours,
GEORGE W. DE HAVEN,
General Manager.

attention, and the performance novel and entertaining by "athletes of very superior order."[8] Smaller cities are more easily satisfied.

Barnum showed them no mercy. His flyers accused the proprietors of advertising his *Congress of Nations*, *Fete at Pekin*, *Donnybrook Fair*, and *Indian Life* in their bills, calling it "fraudulent announcements" by "unscrupulous people." "These parties trade upon my name and reputation," he wrote, "copying verbatim the language used by me ... and other features wholly mine, and produced by me only, and which they do not, can not, and dare not exhibit."[9] In the 1875 Advance Courier he devoted a column to castigate them further. He referred to his imitators as "pigmy swindlers" and "false pretenders" and "little would-be-showmen, with no brains," and "puny tricksters, buying a lot of colored show-bills from the show-printers, and expending not more in their entire outfit than my traveling expenses for two days."

Following the Chicago date, the America's Racing Association worked across the Michigan-Ohio-Indiana triangle and into New York State where it ran into more trouble.[10] It failed to reach Buffalo in time for the morning parade. Then, on the third day of the stand, May 12, another wind of gale force toppled the tent. The unrelenting weather affected a bad condition of the racing course for the entire stay.

The wrath of Barnum, perhaps? No, not really. The entire eastern half of the country was experiencing an unusually frigid April. At mid-month the ice was three feet thick in northern New York. Ten inches of snow fell in New Hampshire; there was frost and ice throughout Tennessee and Mississippi; snow and a temperature of 20° visited Chicago; and just a short distance to the northwest, the mercury was down to zero in Madison, Wisconsin.

The company continued the New York State itinerary on its way to New England. At Albany no performance was given on the afternoon of the May 27 because the sheriff called a halt to operations; but there was an evening show for the benefit of the employees, who in all likelihood had not been receiving their salaries. The show was attached for $16,000, and there were other claims of smaller amounts.[11]

The finale came when the show fell into the hands of the sheriff again at Ogdensburg, New York, on June 11. The property of America's Racing Association was stripped away, piece by piece. Four cages of animals were offered for sale by the *Evening Express* Printing Co. The Albany *Times* reported that another portion of the menagerie, in the shape of three elephants arrived in the city and was seized by the sheriff.

An attempt had been made to spirit them away to Cincinnati but they were detained at East Rochester.

From the start of the season, the show had encountered nearly six weeks where there was scarcely a day that the tents were dry, and consequently the attendance and receipts were small. The establishment being an immense concern and the number of employees large, the expenses were heavy and a plenitude of obligations were incurred. It had been organized with the idea of forestalling Barnum, as the name, style of posters, and many of Barnum's original features were imitated. The plan was to route the show a few weeks in advance of Barnum's Hippodrome, as it worked toward New England where there were already at least five circuses traveling. It "sought to be the first over the northern route and 'scoop' everything else; but it was badly 'worsted,'" a Rochester paper observed.[12]

In October Barnum responded to a report that the America's Racing Association had commenced a suit in Cincinnati against him for injury to their business. He wrote to the *Clipper*:[13]

Bridgeport, Oct. 2, 1875.

Frank Queen, Esq. — Dear Sir: I see by the newspapers that the so called American Racing Association and International Hippodrome have announced that they have sued me in Cincinnati for injuring their business. This is the first that I have heard of it. The fact that they telegraph it to Eastern papers proves that it simply for effect. This concern advertised attractions which they had not got, and nobody but I exhibited. My advertisers exposed them. Their manager then signed an agreement not to do so again, and he and my manager passed receipts in full. This is all there is to it, and it don't amount to shucks.

P. T. Barnum

Barnum's Roman Hippodrome opened under canvas in Philadelphia, at Broad and Norris Streets, for a week on Monday, April 12, which served as the springboard for a six month odyssey throughout the northeastern and middle-western states. Unfortunately, an unexpected cascade of spring rain and snow welcomed the opening night crowd. As one writer put it: "Well-delevoped maidens with low-necked dresses and bare legs may do very well on the stage of the Academy, but when they attempt going through the evolutions of the Amazonian march on damp sawdust the affair loses all glamour of romance, and one cannot help pitying the aforementioned girls or wondering as to the effect upon the cough medicine market."[14]

The first performance opened with the *Fete at Pekin; or, Holiday of the Celestial*. The event is described in the 1875 Advance Courier as:

> Grand Reception of the EMPEROR HAAMTI, A. D. 1690, seated in a Royal Palanquin, borne by Mandarins of the first class, followed by a Grand Procession of Tartar Cavalry, Mongol, Mantchou, and Kathaian Soldiery. Ladies of the Emperor's Court magnificently costumed, carried in elegant Palanquins, resplendent with gold and jewels. Detachment of Lanterns Bearers, with lamps of dazzling brightness. Chusan Officers, carrying elegantly embroidered fans. The chief servants of the Emperor beating gongs. Warriors of the Yantse, with the emblems of the Celestial Empire, THE WINGED DRAGON. Citizen Guards of Pekin, with decorated shields. Disciples of Yung-fut-see, with the Laws of Confucius. Mandarins of the first class bearing spears.
>
> THE FETE
>
> The Emperor, surrounded by his Court, seated beneath the Royal Canopy, adorned with myriads of lanterns, flags and flowers, producing AN ADMIRABLE TOUT ENSEMBLE. Military evolutions by an army of Tartary Cavalry and Chinese Foot Soldiers, PRESENTING A MOVEMENT OF MASS SPLENDOR unparalleled in the annals of spectacular display.
>
> GORGEOUS CHINESE BALLET,
> Consisting of Beautiful Ladies, led by the talented Danseuses,
> M'LLES CARRIE SEYMOUR and MATTIE LEWIS,
> Under the direction of Prof. George Smith.

There was no explanation why *The Congress of Nations* was not used for the opening procession. One must presume that either the weather or the fact that it had been seen in Philadelphia the previous year dictated the change.

The remainder of the program followed the regular pattern with few exceptions. Now, Mme. D'Atalie, in addition to her hazardous chariot racing, was performing her female Samson act, discharging a cannon from her shoulder. The show's ending had been changed to a consolidation of two spectaculer scenes from the pantomime of *Bluebeard*, incorporating the full strength of the company—men, women, and children, richly caparisoned horses, other assorted trained quadrupeds, and "endless paraphernalia incident to the presentation of the great piece." An observer for the *Evening Bulletin* was impressed with the "one hundred and fifty suits of solid silver armor, bedecked and besprinkled with radiance" worn by the women. The armor, he noted, was purchased in London for $75,000 and brought to this country "especially to be shown

Barnum's Great Roman Hippodrome

Advance Courier, 1875

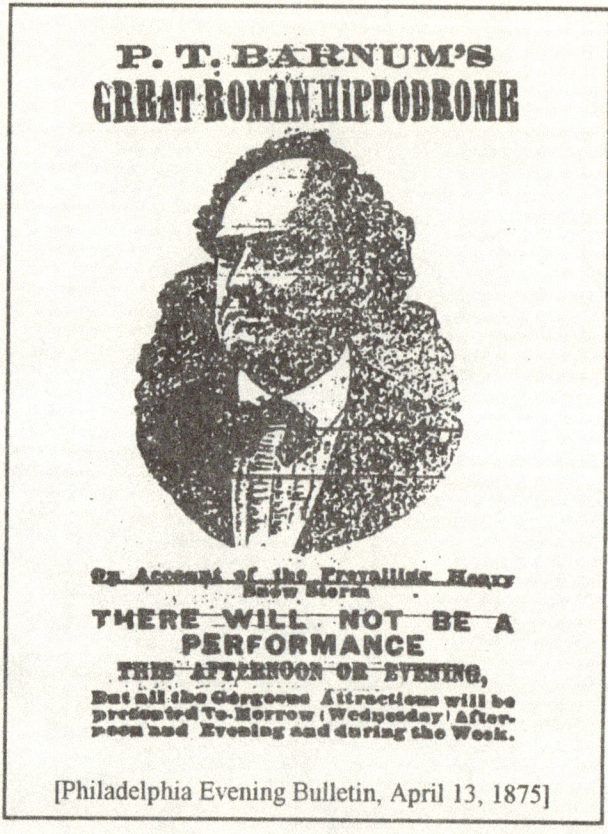

[Philadelphia Evening Bulletin, April 13, 1875]

in this spectacular pageant."[15] But we can be fairly secure in assuming these were the very items Coup bought for his prospective production of *Cinderella* before it was quashed by Barnum.

The weather continued cold and windy throughout the night of the 12th, which was compounded by a sleet and snow storm. The snow intensified until at 6:00 a.m. the tent collapsed from the weight of it. There were about twenty men buried beneath the fallen canvas, all of whom escaped with but slight injury. A center pole was broken, and there was damage to chairs, benches, gas fixtures, etc. The horse tents and workmen's sleeping quarters, a series of smaller tents located on Thirteenth and Norris Streets, suffered no damage.

The severely torn big top necessitated a complete reconstruction. On April 14, fifty sail makers were fast at work repairing tears. On the 15th the managers telegraphed for help from the Higgins tent makers in New York City. Their full crew of sixty workmen arrived at 1:00 p.m. that day and completed the job by 2:00 the following morning. The tent was raised on the 16th and the track repaired. There was a fair house for the matinee that day, but around 6:00 p.m. the snow began to fall again, which ruined the night's business. Saturday, April 17, started off pleasant enough, but by noon the weather changed to a disagreeable cold. On Sunday it snowed all day, forcing the boss canvasman, Charles H. McClean, to lower the canvas. Having given the company a winterland welcome, the weather remained frosty for the rest of the run.

The street parade was not the usual Barnumized event. An advertisement explained: "In consequence of injury that would result to the magnificent wardrobe of Barnum's Hippodrome, if exposed in the streets, and on account of the fact that the lady riders and charioteers cannot endure the fatigue of the street parade, the procession will consist only of the superb band of music, on foot, followed by the blooded race horses, ridden by jockeys." The Barnum people were saving the real flash for inside the tent: "*The Congress of Nations* is not exhibited in the streets. It can only be seen in all its magnificence in the vast amphitheatre."[16]

Donaldson was back with his balloons with plans for daily ascensions to accommodate the local press corps. These trips heavenward cost the management about $500 each. Because of weather conditions and the show being shut down for repairs, the first balloon trip did not occur until Saturday, April 17. The passengers represented the *Evening Bulletin*, the *Press*, the *Times*, and the *Inquirer*. The journey transpired much like the others, followed with the usual and valuable newspaper accounts.

On the 22nd Donaldson made an ascension in a small balloon, capable of holding a single person and ballast. The thing came down near Atco, New Jersey. Three telegrams were sent to Philadelphia, signed by a J. M. Spencer, M.D., stating that Donaldson had been killed by falling out of his craft while still at a great height. Later it was announced that the messages were in error, that the stalwart flier was very much alive. The whole event smelled of "Barnumism." It was later suggested that the wires were sent by Donaldson himself, and that it was all a prearrange publicity ploy for national attention.[17]

The following day, Friday, April 23, the show moved to Newark, New Jersey, for two days. Arrangements had been made with the Newark and Orange Horse Car Company to transport people to and from the show lot, which was bounded by Sussux Avenue and Orange, Third, and Fifth Streets. Cars were scheduled to leave the corner of Broad and Market Streets and from the Clinton Avenue depot at short intervals before both the afternoon and evening performances. Advance tickets purchases were made available at Evans' news depot, 138 Market Street.

Alas! Misfortune shadowed the Hippodrome company along the short jump to Newark. The railway company failed to get the outfit there in time for an afternoon show. But the one at night was well attended with a crowd that began assembling at around 6:00 p.m. At show time the Hippodrome tent was packed to capacity by the 10,000 spectators lucky enough to obtain a seat and by many others who were willing to accept standing room. There were hundreds, it was said, who were unable to obtain admission at all.

Then the following morning snow began to fall and continued until about three inches of it covered the ground. The afternoon balloon ascension did not come off. The brave Donaldson was prepared for the trip, bad weather or no; but the balloon, having been filled by the gas company some distance from the lot, struck a tree in transport and was damaged so badly it was considered unfit for immediate use.

An item in the *Daily Advertiser* offered an interesting portrait of the assemblage on the night of the 24th: "Although on Saturday evening the rain and snow alternately fell thick and fast and a cold wind blew almost a gale, and consequently the immense tent of Barnum's was about as comfortable a place as the most vivid imagination could picture, the ground being wet, the seats not being dry, the vast canvas roof leaking so badly that it seemed as if it were raining harder inside than out, with the thermometer—if there was one in the place—wandering from 25 to 35 degrees, generally keeping close to the first named figure and seldom touching the latter, yet fully five thousand people endured this to see 'the great show.'"[18]

The audience in the half-filled tent, many holding umbrellas, were ushered out before the program was completed. The management, concerned about getting the canvas to the ground lest the snow create havoc similar to the incident in Philadelphia, emptied the tent by 9:30. The sideshow remained opened, however, to cater to the few hardy souls curious enough to observe the scantily dressed Circassian girl wrapped in a blanket and the goosed-bumped "What Is It?" bewildered by his chattering teeth. Yet, despite the fury of the weather, the army of working men tore down the great tent with dispatch, packed everything in its place, and headed for Brooklyn and, hopefully, better conditions.

Following a week in Brooklyn, from April 26 through May 1, the show made one and two-day stands in Connecticut, Massachusetts, Rhode Island, and New York State before moving into Canada. Much like the rival America's Racing Association, disaster seemed to haunt Barnum's Roman Hippodrome, with one accident after another occurring. It was windy and cold all through New England. At New Haven, May 5, Donaldson attempted an ascension in a gale and burst the balloon when he struck a tree. At Hartford the rain made the track so soft that it was impossible to use. At Boston, too, the weather was very cold.

Benton noted in his biography that around the middle of June Barnum and his wife and some English friends paid a visit to Niagara Falls. While they stayed in Buffalo the Hippodrome company arrived. Early in the morning of the show's second day, a special train was arranged by Barnum to treat many of the performers and associates with a trip to the falls. The band was said to have accompanied them across the suspension bridge playing "God Save the Queen" and "Yankee Doodle." The troupe was then returned to Buffalo in time for the afternoon performance.[19] The problem with the story is that the Great Roman Hippodrome did not have Buffalo on its itinerary. It was, however, at nearby St. Catherines, Ontario, for one day on June 18. The visit to the falls, if there was indeed a visit, may have occurred from there.

After leaving Canada, the show was routed through Michigan, Ohio, Indiana, and Illinois before opening in Chicago for a week on July 12. Here, when weather was decent, the mass of humanity that swarmed onto the lot at show time was a sight which amazed even the press people. "Certainly no circus or menagerie that ever visited Chicago has succeeded in arousing such a degree of public interest, and no show of the kind ever drew such enormous audiences," wrote a correspondent for the *Inter-Ocean*. For the first matinee performance, the attendance was in the neighborhood of 9,000 people. At the night show, the house "was packed in every part, more so than on the first night, so that there were probably 15,000 people present."[21]

The large crowd that had assembled for the first balloon ascension on July 14 was disappointed. The balloon had been filled with gas by Chicago's Gas, Light and Coke Company, the bags for ballast contained the highest quality of lake shore sand. Four men stood in the basket as the craft took off—and then came to earth again. A local gas company had failed again. They had agreed to equip the lot with at least a four inch gas input, but when it came time to fill the balloon it was discovered that only a two inch pipe had been laid. So the flight was postponed until the 15th. The delay caused Donaldson his life.

It was noted in the *Inter-Ocean* that Donaldson had made 140 flights in this country, not one ending with any disastrous results: "This will reassure any timid heart, if such there be, among the gentlemen who are desirous to take a birds-eye view of us here below."[22] The balloon sailed from the Chicago Hippodrome exhibition grounds on the lake shore at 4:30 Thursday afternoon, July 15, carrying Donaldson and a single newspaper man from the Chicago *Journal*, N. S. Grimwood. By 7:00 a southwest wind had carried the balloon some thirty miles out over the lake. During the night a tempest swept in from the north.

In retrospect one questions why the balloon was allowed to go up on Thursday. The Barometer had been steadily falling since the 12th. And even before take-off, the balloon was in wretched condition. The cordage that held it to the wicker basket was old and the rents and patches all over the sides of the bag indicated rough treatment and negligence of repairs. The craft had an overall appearance of shabbiness which ought to have deterred the aeronaut from risking his life and the lives of others. In all truth, it was said that Donaldson was reluctant about going up and was in a very nervous state at that time. Why was the balloon not properly maintained? Why was it allowed to fly in this condition? With a failing summer season already eminent, did the management refuse to put out money for a replacement?

On the following evening a coastal schooner brought news of the balloon's peril. The *Little Guide*, a small craft employed in the lumber and tanbark trade, entered the port of Chicago about 9:00 p.m. Upon her arrival her captain, a Swede named Anderssen, told how at about 7:00 on Thursday evening he and his mate, Rasmussen, at some thirty miles from shore had seen the balloon dropping its car once in a while into the lake. Anderssen headed his schooner in that direction, but before he could overtake the machine, which was bounding at a rapid rate on the water, there was a sudden lightening of the car and it shot upward to a great height, soon disappearing altogether. The balloon had apparently lost much of its carrying power, which caused it to hover on

Donaldson's Ascent from the Hippodrome in Chicago [*Harper's Weekly*, August 7, 1875]

the surface of the lake, as it dragged the basket over the crests of the waves.[23] What Donaldson threw overboard to lighten his craft will never be known. But, as the hero of many ascensions, one can be assured that he did all that could be done under the circumstances to save his companion and himself. Barnum viewed him as "a man of excellent habits, clear brains, and steady nerves, fearless, but not reckless, and respected by all who knew him."[24]

By Friday, July 17, the managers of the Hippodrome were still confident that Donaldson and his passenger were safe. The gas that had filled the balloon was sufficient to allow a flight of thirty-six hours. Anyway, precautions had been taken beforehand. Each man was equipped with a life jacket and the balloon's basket was covered with rubber cloth, water-proofing that would allow it to function as a boat if the necessity arose.

Rumors came and went in the ensuing days. One report stated that Donaldson had landed in Grand Haven, Michigan. Another that the balloon had been found by a boat captain and was to be put on exhibition. It was the theory of Samuel A. King, a professional aeronaut from Cleveland, Ohio, that the men had descended into a forest area near the lake, which made it difficult to communicate, but that they would be following the shore line until they found a location where they could. He suggested sending a tug to reconnoiter along the coast. Barnum offered the sum of $500 to anyone finding the bodies. And other agencies contributed small amounts to help cover the cost of the search.

Newton S. Grimwood's body was discovered weeks later, on Monday, August 16, by a mail carrier, Alanson Beckwith. It had washed up at a place on the lake shore called Stoney Point, about two miles south of Benona, Michigan, a small lumber-milling settlement, and twelve miles north of Montague. A broken life preserver was wrapped about his neck. There were no boots on his feet. His watch had stopped at 11:20.

There were a number of fabrications about Donaldson still being alive, since his body was never found. The Des Moines *Register* published an item about a nut named Jackson who claimed that Donaldson had made an ascent in that city under the alias of "Sailor Ned." He insisted he had had a conversation with the famous aeronaut and learned from him that, it being impossible for both men to be saved, Donaldson had cut the basket loose with a hatchet, leaving Grimwood to drown, while he sailed away and landed on the Lake Michigan shore and later joined the Hippodrome company in disguise, where he remained. A note found in a bottle and supposedly bearing Donaldson's signature was discovered on the lake shore and submitted to W. C. Coup for authentication. Coup deemed it to be a forgery but forwarded it to S. H. Hurd, who was more familiar with Donaldson's handwriting. In Evansville, Indiana, a man questioned one of the Hippodrome associates, "Where is Wash Donaldson?" After further inquiry, he stated, "My cousin is a relative of Donaldson's, and he says he saw him here tonight." This kind of refusal to accept the death of a celebrated person happens frequently, but there were many who suspected another Barnum "humbug" as being behind the publicity of Donaldson's disappearance.

St. Louis was next on the itinerary, visited for six days beginning July 19. The tents, occupying three blocks, were situated on the south side of Spruce between Eighth and Eleventh Streets. Although it required substantial grading to bring it level enough to accommodate the hippodrome track, the lot was an important location, in close proximity to streetcars running from almost every part of the city. The Fifth Street cars, the Gravois Road cars, the Union Depot and Lafayette Park Line, all passed within a block; while Fourth Street, Market Street, and the Blue Line, were within easy walking distance.

The man writing for the *Globe-Democrat* thought the races were the most appealing part of the program, there being no gambling or trickery to interfere with the result. "These races rouse the audience to a great pitch of excitement, and they cheer horses and riders with shouts of encouragement as they speed around the track." He found the horses all good, "some of them splendid animals, and the ladies ... graceful and accomplished riders."[25]

The immediate replacement for the lost Donaldson was none other than D. S. Thomas. The intrepid press agent made a single ascension in Chicago directly following the accident. He made his second flight as master of the *Barnum No. 4* in St. Louis on Tuesday the 20th. This balloon, perhaps the only one remaining, had a 26,000 cubic foot capacity. After lift-off he rose to 4,700 feet, floated in a southeasterly direction, and landed in Illinois, a mile east of the Mississippi River. Since there was plenty of gas left in the bag, he made another ascent to a 4,300 foot level. This time he came down near Belleville, Illinois. He took off for a third time, staying aloft for two hours before landing successfully seven miles east of Belleville at about 9:00 p.m. of the same day.[26]

From St. Louis the show made an extensive swing through Illinois, Iowa, Minnesota, Wisconsin, stretching as far west as Omaha and as far south as Louisville. Making their way west, a flood followed them through the state of Iowa, where at times it was impossible to get the tents up. After leaving the flood area, they made their way east through Missouri, Indiana, and Ohio. A spirited state election in the latter distracted much of the public.[20] The tour ended with a stand at Cleveland on the corner of Superior and Perry Streets, October 7, 8, and 9. Here, as at many of the previous places, excursion trains made it convenient for people in the outlying communities to get to the matinees. The Lake Shore & Michigan railway sold round trip tickets from Elyria, Painesville, and intermediate stations. The Cleveland & Pittsburgh gave service from Ravenna and points north, and on Saturday as far as Alliance. The Bee Line operated at half-rates on Saturday only from Galion and stations north. Also on Saturday, the Atlantic & Great Western sold half-fare tickets from Warrenton and intermediate stations. With each of these transportation units, a coupon of admission to the Hippodrome was included, saving riders the inconvenience of purchasing tickets at the crowded show grounds.

The 1875 summer season ended being one of the worst in the history of traveling amusements. Of the thirty-six or more shows that set forth in the spring, half of them collapsed before fall. Although the Hippodrome company finished out its tour, it closed in the red. Barnum, in typical over-statement, called it "a tolerably successful season, notwithstanding the depressed state of finances generally."[27] Dingess tells us that W. C. Coup, feeling that Barnum himself was more to blame than anyone else for the loss, refused to continue in the enterprise, having fully determined the spring before to withdraw. Coup paid for his share of the deficit and that of Castello; Barnum paid his for own and for his ex-son-in-law, Hurd.[28] Charles H. Day suggested that Hurd, Bunnell, and Coup "got badly pinched," and that Castello went out broke and never recovered.[29] Thus ended their famous partnership. Although rumors of a tiff between Barnum and Coup have existed for years, in all fairness, Coup has not made a public statement to this effect and, indeed, it may not be true.

In justifying the failure of the 1875 season, we have seen that ill weather played a major role, and, of course, the financial depression which was to continue for a few more years. We also might look back to a mid-season observation by a reporter from a Chicago paper who stated: "The country folk are slow to endorse innovations, and in many rural districts, no doubt, the absence of their familiar friend, the clown, and the substitution of live actual racing for the old feats of bareback riding, is still regarded with distrust."[30] The bottom line has to be that the traveling Hippodrome was simply too big, too expensive, and too extravagantly managed to prosper within the pattern of a circus, performing in the smaller towns and moving daily for the most part, all for front door admission prices of 50¢ and 25¢.

The great expectation that had been articulated when Barnum's Universal Exposition Company was chartered in 1874 to have a score or more exhibitions, traveling and permanent, in American and Europe, did not materialize. Mid-season advertisements included "Its Last and Only Tour on This Continent," and revealed that arrangements had been made to take the entire Hippodrome to Europe, with an opening in London at Christmas time. Even at the last stand in Cleveland, a European tour was apparently being considered; for on October 8 the *Plain Dealer* announced: "From here, at the greatest expense ever undertaken by a management, the hippodrome will be shipped direct to London."

The change of fortune brought on by the summer's failure and, perhaps, the disenchantment of his partners, discouraged Barnum's European designs. In addition, as far back as 1873 he had envisioned a balloon Atlantic crossing as a means of publicizing a continental tour. With Donaldson gone and no real scientific discoveries to assure the success of such a flight, the scheme was abandoned. Still, Barnum had hopes of shipping the show to South America and had advertised for a partner.[31] But, alas, no man of money surfaced.

Plans were then announced for disposal of the property. Both the Roman Hippodrome and the World's Fair were put up for sale, beginning on Monday, November 26. The attendance on that day was disappointing, the weather being unfavorable, but included some major circus figures—W. W. Cole, J. J. Nathans, Avery Smith, George F. Bailey, Walter Waterman, Hyatt Frost, John Murray, James Melville, Ben Maginley, E. D. Colvin, Levi J. North, Egbert Howes, Henry D. Palmer, A. A. Stewart (representing Old John Robinson)—some of whom, no doubt, had come to witness the spectacle and visit with old friends. Much of the paraphernalia and costumes was sold by boxes which were displayed upon seats within the Hippodrome building. They contained such items as band uniforms, jeweled armor, wigs, banners, the Lord Mayor of London's coach (which brought a mere $60). The whole of things went for less than $5,000. The silver armor and harness were sold the following day. The rest of the equipment and stock were disposed of in Bridgeport on the 29th and 30th. The animals to be auctioned off were put on exhibition prior to that date and admission prices of 25¢ and 15¢ entitled the curious locals to browse amongst Barnum's collection of beasts.[32] With that, the Great Roman Hippodrome, like its ancient forerunner, was in ruins.

NOTES

[1] Barnum, *Selected Letters*, p. 190.
[2] Dubuque *Herald*, August 13, 1875. The paper stated that the troupe personnel filled 59 railroad cars.
[3] Clipping, Syracuse *Morning Standard*, June 10, 1875, quoting from the New York *Sun*, April 12, 1875 (n.p.n.).
[4] Clipping, Walworth County *Liberal*, April 10, 1875, quoting *Harper's Weekly* (n.p.n.).
[5] New York *Clipper* Supplement, April 17, 1875.
[6] New York Clipper, April 24, 1875.
[7] New York *Clipper*, May 8, 1875.
[8] New York *Clipper*, May 29, 1875.
[9] Copy of handbill at the Robert L. Parkinson Library and Research Center, from the Don S. Howland collection.
[10] The projected itinerary was South Bend, IN, May 3; Kalamazoo, MI, 4; Jackson, 5; Detroit, 6, 7; Toledo, OH, 8; Buffalo, NY, 10-12; Lockport, 13; Rochester, 14, 15; Auburn, 18; Albany 24, 25; Troy, 26; Cohoes, 27; Saratoga Springs, 28; Whitehall, 29. Later changed to Cohoes, 31; Schenectady, June 1. As is stated, this changed following the Albany date.
[11] New York *Clipper*, June 5, 1875.
[12] Rochester (NY) *Daily Union and Advertiser*, May 17, 1875.
[13] New York *Clipper*, October 16, 1875.
[14] Philadelphia *Evening Bulletin*, April 13, 1875.
[15] *Ibid.*
[16] Clipping of advertisement for the Janesville, Wisconsin, stand of August 24.
[17] New York *Clipper*, May 1, 1875.
[18] Newark *Daily Advertiser*, April 26, 1875.
[19] Joel Benton, *Life of Hon. Phineas T. Barnum*, p. 505.
[20] Dingess manuscript, p. 373.
[21] Clipping, Chicago *Inter-Ocean*, July 14, 1875.
[22] *Ibid.* Barnum stated in his autobiography that this final ascension was Prof. Donaldson's 138th.
[23] *Harper's Weekly*, August 7, 1875.

[24] Barnum, *Struggles and Triumphs*, 1927 edition, p. 718.
[25] Clipping, St. Louis *Globe-Democrat*, September 9, 1875.
[26] Galesburg (IL) *Republican-Register*, July 31, 1875, reprinted from the St. Louis *Globe-Democrat*, July 22, 1875.
[27] Barnum, *Struggles and Triumphs*, 1927 edition, p. 718.
[28] Dingess, *op. cit.*
[29] Day, *Ink from a Circus Press Agent*, p. 90.
[30] Clipping, Chicago *Inter-Ocean*, July 14, 1875. Benton, in his biography of Barnum, wrote that the season was "a fairly profitable one."
[31] New York *Clipper*, November 13, 1875.
[32] New York *Clipper*, November 27, December 4, December 11, 1875.

CONCLUSIONS AND SPECULATIONS

P. T. Barnum's entrance into the circus business marked the beginning of a new era for tented attractions. The drawing power of the Barnum name and the skillful use of it during the early years of the postwar decade brought financial gain and innovative change. The management combination of Barnum, Coup, Castello, and Hurd appears to have worked well, with each man contributing a fair share within individual areas of aptitude. Although Barnum was not closely involved in the day-to-day operations, his surrogate and financial lookout, S. H. Hurd, must have kept him well informed.

We can clearly perceive the Barnum hand in the advertising style. He is said to have supervised every line of the stock letter press that was composed during the winter. A prolific letter writer, he sent out missiles ahead of the show to both newspaper editors and local clergy, touting the moral and educational values exhibited within his canvas temples. A contemporary, press agent Charles H. Day, called him a "constant suggester," continually supplying his press people with hints written down on bits of paper, envelopes, or whatever was handy at wherever he was composing it.[1]

Barnum had little interest in the circus as a performing entity. Consistent with his prudish nature, he may even have been embarrassed by its tawdry image in the minds of a large portion of the public; for within the years covered in this volume, the word "Circus" was not included in his show titles. In the advertising and on the pages of his couriers, the acts took a secondary position to the oddities and animals.

Indeed, his chief interest was in accumulating exhibits to add to the museum and menagerie, for which he spent large sums. His fearlessness in doling out money, although troublesome to his partners, was a major contribution to the show's success. He had the greatest level of expectation that whatever he spent would return two-fold than any proprietor of his time.

It can be said that W. C. Coup and Dan Castello did not receive their share of credit from a universal audience for successfully guiding the so-called Barnum shows during their five-year tenure. The seed of sprouting Barnum into circusdom originated with them. It took a good deal of persuasion—and perhaps flattery—to entice the aging legend into lending his name to their project. If all they received from Barnum was his name, as was their original intent, it is likely the pair would have still succeeded. But with the name came Barnum's money, his penchant for impressive display, and an apparent unwillingness to share the limelight.

His exorbitant spending, although instrumental in attracting audiences, must have complicated the management process. It created an imperative for continually enlarging the spread of canvas to accommodate the crowds; and with that came the need for more equipment and more personnel—and more headaches. And, to the credit of Coup and Castello, the necessity for rapid growth produced valuable innovations to the formerly unchanging nature of circus operation.

Yet Barnum could not bring himself to say "we." In his autobiography—in general, a tome of self-aggrandizement—he makes no mention of Coup and Castello's part in the origins of "the greatest show on earth." Rather, he tells us that in order to "open a safety-valve" for his "pent-up energies" he began to "prepare a great show enterprise."[2] In expounding on the success of the first season, he refers to Coup as "my manager" and makes no mention of Castello. Taking sole credit for the move to rail travel, his brief but glowing account of the second season's accomplishments ignores his partners completely. We might remind the reader that it was Barnum's "manager", a twenty percent owner of the enterprise, who had so diligently and strenuously devoted himself to the operation of the show that it became necessary for him to go abroad in the spring of 1874 for a short rest, until Barnum summoned him home.

There is no evidence to indicate that either Coup or Castello complained about their relationship with Barnum through any public forum, just as there is nothing to verify the presence of any discontent. But one has to wonder. Here are two experienced and capable showmen, involved in the day-to-day problems of a large circus operation, made subordinate to the celebrity of the self-righteous Barnum. The explanation has to be that they were shrewdly aware of the drawing power of the Barnum name and were willing to put up with most any inconvenience or denigration so long as it led to success.

Coup and Castello were meticulous in their planning. In the very first year on the road their outfit was larger than anything yet attempted. With nothing more than an ordinary performing troupe, they used the drawing power of their immense museum and liberal assortment of exotic animals. At the outset, they demonstrated to other circus managers that, with proper handling, a large and expensive show could make money. When visiting the smaller towns, they billed for forty and fifty miles in every direction, attracting people from greater distances than ever before. They adjusted to the need for increased seating by enlarging the canvas at various times; and with the enlargement came the adoption of a second ring. When the show went to rail transportation, they perfected a means of loading and unloading the cars with efficiency. They developed a systematic method of setting up and tearing down the outfit with the minimum of labor and within the minimum time. They were overseers of a show the size of which no other American proprietor had ever experienced.

Still, much credit must be attributed to the Barnum name and the Barnum skill in publicizing an amusement. No other circus proprietor of his day had his capacity for acquiring newspaper space. His display advertisements, which he certainly had control over, were bold, extravagant, and over-blown. Frequently comprising two columns, or as much as a full page, they were adorned with the easily identifiable likeness of the "Prince of Humbug" himself, a kind of copyright logo to assure the public that this was indeed a genuine P. T. Barnum enterprise. Copy contributed by the local papers was copious when compared to the scant notices given to rival circuses. Charles H. Day said of him: "During Barnum's entire career he was ever writing and suggesting and was particularly strong in cards, statements and proclamations."[3] When the show met stiff opposition, Barnum's managers encouraged him to come forward and lend his weighty reputation to the fray. Upon his arrival, he was interviewed and editorialized and frequently idolized like a Hollywood hero by star struck local editors.

With Barnum, as with no other circus impresario, the public seemed willing to accept the contradiction between his moral philanthropy and the "catch-penny clap-trap," as one writer phrased it—lecturing on temperance "to those who were already practicing it, while his main efforts [were] devoted to cultivating the taste of Young America for horse-racing and savage sports."[4] Certainly one must distinguish between the Barnum who posed as a public servant and the man who cleverly acquired a fortune by deceiving the same public with inflated advertisements and blatant "humbuggery."

It is difficult to call the decision to produce the Great Roman Hippodrome a mistake. Certainly the first New York season and the limited tour to the handful of selected cities was profitable. It was a project that only the Barnum name could carry off, given the economic climate of the time. Extending the mammoth exhibition another year, however, and attempting to move it about in the manner of the traditional circus, proved to be an error in judgment or just plain bad luck. If any one of the parties involved can be faulted, it would have to be Barnum, who clearly had the final word in money matters. He appears to have been seeking approval from a broader audience for his "crowning effort," and in so doing was bitten by the financial wolf.

Then there was what has later been called an unexplainable union between Barnum and John "Pogey" O'Brien. With his attention focused on the Hippodrome, Barnum was left with unused circus property. He opted to keep it on the road and collect the income, selecting O'Brien as a co-proprietor or lessee; the financial arrangement has never been made clear. Why he placed his circus in the hands of this man has been seen by pundits as a conundrum. It is apparent that he was sensitive about it from the lengthy and over-reactive card placed in the New York *Clipper* during March of 1874. It began: "Every spring a report is circulated by envious and unsuccessful mountebanks—not showmen—with all the unscrupulous and reckless persistence jealous malice can beget, that 'Barnum has hired out his name.'" It goes on to call these claims a "shameful and groundless falsehood." His detractors are labeled "tricky scandalmongers." "I am remorseless," he states, "in my determination to wage a war of utter extermination against the entire horde of character and credit assassins, who aim their mercenary stabs at the purity and beneficent purpose of popular entertainments, between which and them I have taken a final, and, so far, not an altogether unsuccessful stand, as the annihilation of some of the worst of them, and the sore scorching of many others, gratifyingly indicate."[5] Yet, in spite of such self-righteous phrases, he turned his Great Traveling World's Fair over to the superintendence of O'Brien, who, throughout a lengthy career in management, developed a reputation of dishonesty, coarseness, and a tolerance for grifters.

But let us try to find the answer to this. By 1874, John O'Brien had been in management for ten years, longer than either Coup or Castello before they teamed with Barnum. For all we know, O'Brien's negative reputation had not surfaced at this point. At thirty-eight years of age he was young and experienced in the business. In 1870 he had a fifty cage menagerie attached to his circus, the largest in the country. The following year he had accumulated so much property that he put four outfits on the road, each with a menagerie.[6] This penchant for collecting animals must have impressed Barnum. According to lion tamer George Conklin, who had worked for him during the 1860s, O'Brien "was one of those unique and successful characters not uncommon in this country during the first five or six decades of the nineteenth century."[7] In the three years prior to taking out a show under Barnum's name, he was looked upon as one of the most successful circus managers in the country. He neither smoked nor drank and had built a career from humble beginnings through shrewdness and shrift, which certainly appealed to his prim and proper co-proprietor. With such a resume, who else had as an impressive a record, was available and as qualified?

The Barnum/O'Brien relationship terminated with the end of the 1875 season and the auctioning off of show stock and equipment. The major buyers were the "Flatfoots," Avery Smith (who died shortly thereafter), John Nathans, George F. Bailey, and Lewis June. These associates became the new operators of a circus under the Barnum name. The arrangement lasted for five seasons before—faced with declining profits and increased competition—the aging Barnum capitulated to the ingenious tactics of a young upstart named James A. Bailey. In 1881 the two men combined their circuses; and for the first time, the name of P. T. Barnum was shared in a show title with others, making it the great double company of Barnum, Bailey & Hutchinson.

NOTES

[1] Day, *Ink from a Circus Press Agent*, p. 126.
[2] Barnum, *Struggles and Triumphs*, p. 681.
[3] Day, *op. cit.*, p. 6.
[4] Newark *Daily Advertiser*, April 26, 1875, p. 2.
[5] New York *Clipper*, March 21, 1874, p. 405.
[6] John O'Brien's Caravan, Monster Menagerie and National Kingdom; Sheldenberger's European Menagerie and Grecian Circus; Hardenberger & Co.'s Circus; J. E. Warner & Co.'s Great Pacific Menagerie and Circus.
[7] George Conklin, *The Ways of the Circus*, p. 23.

THE BARNUM ROUTE FROM 1871 THROUGH 1875

P. T. Barnum's Museum, Menagerie and Circus, 1871
Apr. 10—15, Brooklyn, NY. (Fulton Ave., near Hoyt St.)
SUNDAY
17-Greenpoint, NY.
18—19-Williamsburg, NY.
20—21-Jersey City, NJ
22-Hoboken, NJ.
SUNDAY
24-Paterson, NJ.
25-Plainfield, NJ.
26-Morristown, NJ.
27-Elizabeth, NJ.
28—29-Newark, NJ.
SUNDAY

MAY
1-Hudson City, NJ.
2-Mott Haven NY.
3-White Plains, NY.
4-Stamford, CT.
5-Norwalk, CT.
6-Danbury, CT.
SUNDAY
8-Bridgeport, CT.
9-Derby, CT.
10-New Haven, CT.
11-Waterbury, CT.
12-Meriden, CT.
13-New Britain, CT.
SUNDAY
15—16-Hartford, CT.
17-Rockville, CT.
18-Springfield, MA.
19-Chicopee, MA.
20-Holyoke, MA.
SUNDAY
22-Northampton, MA.
23-Ware, MA.
24-Southbridge, MA.
25-Danielson, CT.
26-Norwich, CT.
27-New London, CT.
SUNDAY
29-Westerly, RI.
30-Brand Iron Works, RI.
31-Phenix, RI.

JUNE
1-East Greenwich, RI.
2—3-Providence, RI.
SUNDAY
5-Fall River, MA.
6-New Bedford, MA.
7-Middleboro, MA.
8-Plymouth, MA.
9-Abington, MA.
10-Quincy, MA.
SUNDAY
12—17-Boston, MA (Fair Grounds)
SUNDAY
19-Roxbury, MA.
20-South Boston, MA.
21-Cambridgeport, MA.
22-East Boston, MA.
23-Chelsea, MA.
24-Lynn, MA.
SUNDAY
26-Gloucester, MA.
27-Salem, MA.
29-Newburyport, MA.
29-Haverhill, MA.
30-Lawrence, MA.

JULY
1-Nashua, NH.
SUNDAY
3—4-Lowell, MA.
5-Natick. MA.
6-Milford, MA.
7-Marlboro, MA.

8-Worcester, MA.
SUNDAY
10-Fitchburg, MA.
11-Winchendon, MA.
12-Athol, MA.
13-Greenfield, MA.
14-Brattleboro, VT.
15-Keene, NH.
SUNDAY
17-Peterboro, NH.
18-Milford, NH.
19-Manchester, NH.
20-Exeter, NH.
21-Portsmouth, NH.
22-Dover, NH.
SUNDAY
24-Saco, ME.
25-Portland, ME.
26-Brunswick, ME.
27-Gardiner, ME.
28-Augusta, ME.
29-Waterville, ME.
SUNDAY
31-Lewistown, ME.

AUGUST
1-Paris, ME.
2-Bridgeton, ME.
3-Conway, NH.
4-Wolfeboro, NH.
5-Laconia, NH.
SUNDAY
7-Lebanon, NH.
8-Claremont, NH.
9-Ludlow, VT.
10-Rutland, VT.
11-Whitehall, NY.
12-Glens Falls, NY.

SUNDAY
14-Saratoga Springs, NY.
15-Schuylerville, NY.
16-Salem, NY.
17-Hoosick, NY.
18-Bennington, VT.
19-Williamstown, MA.
SUNDAY
21-Troy, NY.
22—23-Albany, NY.
24-Schenectidy, NY.
25-Ballston Spa, NY.
26-Amsterdam, NY.
SUNDAY
Johnstown, NY.
29-Ft. Plain, NY.
30-Little Falls, NY.
31-Utica, NY.

SEPTEMBER
1-Rome, NY.
2-Camden, NY.
SUNDAY
4-Oswego, NY.
5-Fulton, NY.
6—7-Syracuse, NY.
8-Auburn, NY.
9-Moravia, NY.
SUNDAY
11-Cortland. NY.
12-Ithica, NY.
13-Ovid, NY.
14-Seneca Falls, NY.
15-Clyde, NY.
16-Palmyra, NY.
SUNDAY
18—19-Rochester, NY.
20-Albion, NY.
21-Madina, NY.
22-Lockport, NY.
23-Niagara Falls, NY.
SUNDAY
25—26-Buffaalo, NY.
27-Aurora, NY.
28-Attica, NY.
29-Batavia. NY.
30-Le Roy, NY.
SUNDAY

OCTOBER
2-Canandaigua, NY.
3-Penn Yan, NY.
4-Watkins, NY.
5-Corning, NY.
6-Elmira, NY.
7-Waverly, NY.
SUNDAY
9-Owego, NY.
10-Binghamton, NY.
11-Greene, NY.
12-Norwich, NY.
13-Unadilla, NY.
14-Oneonta, NY.
SUNDAY
16-Cooperstown, NY.

17-Cobleskill, NY
18-Middleburg, NY.
19-Cairo, NY.
20-Catskill, NY.
21-Kingston, NY.
SUNDAY
23-Pouthkeepsie, NY.
24-Newburgh, NY.
25-Peekskill, NY.
26-Sing Sing, NY.
27-Yonkers, NY.
28-Harlem, NY.
SUNDAY
OCT. 30—NOV. 11, at rest, NYC.
SUNDAY
NOV. 13 (Night)— JAN. 6-NYC (Empire Rink, 63rd St. and 3rd Ave.)
Winter Quarters, NYC.

P. T. Barnum's Traveling Exposition and World's Fair, 1872.

Apr. 1—13-NYC (Empire Rink, 3rd Ave. and 63rd St., night opening)
SUNDAY
15-Jersey City, NJ.
16-Newark, NJ.
17-Elizabeth, NJ.
18-New Brunswick, NJ.
19-Trenton, NJ.
20-Camden, NJ.
SUNDAY
22—27-Philadelphia, PA.
SUNDAY
29-Chester, PA.
30-Wilmington, DE.

MAY
1—4-Baltimore, MD.
SUNDAY
6—7-Washington, DC.
8-Frederick, MD.
9-Hagerstown, MD.
10-Chambersburg, PA.
11-Carlisle, PA.
SUNDAY
13-Harrisburg, PA.
14-York, PA.
15-Lancaster, PA.
16-Reading, PA.
17-Pottsville, PA.
18-Allentown, PA.
SUNDAY
20-Easton, PA.
21-Lehighton, PA.
22-Wilkes-Barre, PA.
23-Scranton, PA.
24-Danville, PA.
25-Williamsport, PA.
SUNDAY
27-Lock Haven, PA.
28-Altoona, PA.
29-Johnstown, PA.
May 30—June 1, Allegheny, PA. (Pittsburgh)
SUNDAY

JUNE
3-Wheeling, WV.
4-Steubenville, OH.
5-New Castle, PA.
6-Sharon, PA.
7-Erie, PA.
8-Corry, PA.
SUNDAY
10-Jamestown, NY.
11-Titusville, PA.
12-Oil City, PA.
13-Meadville, PA.
14-Warren, OH.
15-Akron, OH.
SUNDAY
17—18-Cleveland, OH.
19-Alliance, OH.
20-Canton, OH.
21-Massillon, OH.
22-Mansfield. OH.
SUNDAY
24-Mt. Vernon, OH.
25-Newark, OH.
26-Zanesville, OH.
27-Lancaster, OH.
28-Columbus, OH.
29-Delaware, OH.
SUNDAY

JULY
1-Springfield, OH.
2-Bellefontaint, OH.
3-Tiffin, OH.
4-Sandusky, OH.
5-Fremont, OH.
6-Monroe, MI.
SUNDAY
9-Adrian, MI.
9-Toledo, OH.
10-Lima, OH.
11-Piqua, OH.
12-Dayton, OH.
13-Hamilton, OH.
SUNDAY
15-Richmond, IN.
16—19-Cincinnati, OH.
20-Covington, KY.
SUNDAY
22-Aurora, IN.
23-Jeffersonville, IN.
24—25-Louisville, KY.
26-New Albany, IN.
27-Columbus, IN.
SUNDAY
29—30-Indianapolis, IN.
31-Terre Haute, IN.

AUGUST
1-Vincennes, IN.
2-Evansville, IN.
3-Washington, IN.
SUNDAY
5—10-St. Louis, MO.
SUNDAY
12-Jefferson City, MO.
13-Sedalia, MO.
14-Kansas City, MO.
15-Topeka, KS.
16-Lawrence, KS.
17-Leavenworth, KS.
SUNDAY
19-Atchison, KS.
20-St. Joseph, MO.
21-Chillicothe, MO.
22-Macon, MO.
23-Hannibal, MO.
24-Quincy, IL.
SUNDAY
26-Burlington, IA.
27-Galesburg, IL.
28-Peoria, IL.
29-Bloomington, IL.
30-Decatur, IL.
31-Springfield, IL.
SUNDAY

SEPTEMBER
2-Jacksonville, IL.
3-Mt. Sterling, IL.
4-Keokuk, IA.
5-Ottumwa, IA.
6-Oskaloosa, IA.
7-Des Moines, IA.
SUNDAY
9-Iowa City, IA.
10-Davenport, IA.
11-Clinton, IA.
12-Freeport, IL.
13-Dubuque, IA.
14-Waterloo. IA.
SUNDAY
16-Owatonna. MN.
17-Minneapolis, MN.
18-19-St. Paul, MN.
20-Winona, MN.
21-LaCosse, WI.
SUNDAY
23-Madison, WI.
24-Rockford, IL.
25-Elgin, IL.
26-Janesville, WI.
27-Fond du Lac, WI.
28-Green Bay, WI.
SUNDAY
30-Neenah, WI.

OCTOBER
1-Oshkosh, WI.
2-Watertown, WI.
3—4-Milwaukee, WI.
5-Racine, WI.
SUNDAY
7—10-Chicago, IL.
11-Aurora, IL.
12-Ottawa, IL.
SUNDAY
14-Joliet, IL.
15-Kankakee, IL.
17-Danville, IL.
18-Lafayette, IN.
19-Logansport, IN.
SUNDAY
21-Ft.Wayne, IN.
22-Sturgis, MI.
23-Grand Rapids,

MI.
24-Kalamozoo, MI.
25-Marshall, MI.
26-Jackson, MI.
SUNDAY
28-Ann Arbor, MI.
29—31-Detroit, MI.
Oct. 31—Nov. 9, en route
SUNDAY

NOVEMBER
11—16-at rest, NYC. (Nov. 11 opening postponed due to sick horses)
SUNDAY
18 (night)—23- NYC, Hippotheatron, 14th St. Season ended by fire which destroyed the Hippotheatron, 4:00 a.m., Wednesday, Dec. 24.

P. T. Barnum's Great Traveling Exposition and World's Fair, 1873.
Mar. 29 (afternoon)— Apr. 15-NYC (American Institute, 63rd and 3rd)

APRIL
16-19-Brooklyn (Capitoline Grounds)
SUNDAY
21-Norwalk, CT.
22-Bridgeport, CT.
23-Waterbury, CT.
24—25-New Haven, CT.
26-Meriden, CT.
SUNDAY
28—29-Hartford, CT.
30-Northampton, MA.

MAY
1-Springfield, MA.
2-Worcester, MA.
3-Woonsocket, MA.
SUNDAY
5—6-Providence, RI.
7-Taunton-MA.
8-New Bedford, MA.
9-Fall River, MA.
10-North Bridgewater, MA.
SUNDAY
12—22-Boston, MA.
23-Salem, MA.
24-Lynn, MA.

SUNDAY
26-Glouster, MA.
27-Portsmouth, NH.
28-Portland, ME.
29-Lewiston, ME.
30-Saco, ME.
31-Dover, NH.
SUNDAY

JUNE
2-Haverhill, MA.
3-Lawrence, MA.
4-Manchester, NH.
5-Concord, NH.
6-Lowell, MA.
7-Fitchburg, MA.
SUNDAY
9-Pittsfield, MA.
10—11-Albany. NY.
12-Troy, NY.
13-Ft. Edwards, NY.
14-Rutland, VT.
SUNDAY
16-Burlington, VT.
17-St. Albans, VT.
18-Malone, NY.
19-Ogdensburg, NY.
20-Watertown, NY.
21-Utica, NY.
SUNDAY
23-Oswego, NY.
24-Syracuse, NY.
25-Auburn, NY.
26-Canandiagua, NY.
27—28-Rochester,

NY.
SUNDAY
30-Lockport, NY.

JULY
1—2-Buffalo, NY.
3-Dunkirk, NY.
4-Corry, PA.
5-Titusville, PA.
SUNDAY
7—10-Pittsburgh, PA.
11-Rochester, PA.
12-Youngstown, OH.
SUNDAY
14—16-Cleveland, OH.
17-Galion, OH.
18-Columbus, OH.
19-Springfield, OH.
SUNDAY
21—24-Cincinnati, OH.
25-Hamilton, OH.
26-Dayton, OH.
SUNDAY
28—29-Indianapolis, IN.
30-Lafayette, IN.
31-Danville, IL.

AUGUST
1-Terre Haute, IN.
2-Mattoon, IL.
SUNDAY
4—9-St. Louis, MO.
SUNDAY
11-Decatur, IL.
12-Springfield, IL.
13-Jacksonville, IL.
14-Peoria, IL.
15-Bloomington, IL.
16-Joliet, IL.
SUNDAY
18—23-Chicago, IL.
SUNDAY
25-LaPorte, IN.
26-South Bend, IN.
27-Coldwater, MI.
28-Adrian, MI.
29-Toledo, OH.
30-Jackson, MI.
SUNDAY

SEPTEMBER
1-Grand Rapids, MI.
2-Lansing, MI.
3-East Saginaw, MI.
4-Flint, MI.
5—6-Detroit, MI.
SUNDAY
8-London, Ont.
9-Brantford, Ont.
10-Hamilton, Ont.
11—12-Toronto, Ont.
13-St. Catharines, Ont.
SUNDAY
15-Batavia, NY.
16-Penn Yan, NY.
17-Elmira, NY.
18-Williamsport, PA.
19-Sunbury, PA.
20-Harrisburg, PA.
SUNDAY
22—25-Baltimore, MD.
26—27-Washington, DC.
SUNDAY
Sept. 29—Oct. 4-Philadelphia, PA.
SUNDAY

OCTOBER
6-Trenton, NJ.
7-Elizabeth, NJ.
8—9-Newark, NJ.
10—11-Jersey City, NJ.
SUNDAY
13—18-Brooklyn, NY (Capitoline Grounds)
SUNDAY
Oct. 20 (night)—Nov. 15-NYC Hippodrome (26th and Madison)

P. T. Barnum's Great Roman Hippodrome, 1874
Apr. 27—Aug. 1-NYC Hippodrome (26th and

Madison)
SUNDAY
Aug. 3 (night)—
  Aug. 22-Boston,
  MA. (foot of
  Boylston St.)
SUNDAY

AUGUST-SEPTEMBER
24-en route
25 (night)—Sept.
  11-Philadelphia

SEPTEMBER
12-en route
SUNDAY
14—26-Baltimore
  (night opening;
  a.m. and p.m.
  shows on 25th in
  lieu of p.m. and
  night)
SUNDAY
28-en route
29 (night)—Oct. 10-
  Pittsburgh
  (Union Park,
  Allegheny)
SUNDAY

OCTOBER
12-en route
13 (night)—24-
  Cincinnati
  (Lincoln Park)
SUNDAY
26—31-en route
SUNDAY

NOV.-JANUARY
2 (Night)—Jan. 2,
  NYC
  Hippodrome

P. T. Barnum's Great Roman Hippodrome, 1875

Mar. 29
  (afternoon)—
  April 10, NYC
  Hippodrome
SUNDAY

APRIL-MAY
12—22,
  Philadelphia,
  PA.
23—24-Newark,
  NJ.
SUNDAY
26—May 1-
  Brooklyn, NY
  (Capitoline
  Grounds)

MAY
SUNDAY
3-Bridgeport, CT.
4—5-New Haven,
  CT.
6—7-Hartford, CT.
8-Springfield, MA.
SUNDAY
10—11-Worcester,
  MA.

12—14-Providence,
  RI.
15-Taunton, MA.
SUNDAY
17—27-Boston,
  MA.
28—29-Lynn, MA.
SUNDAY
31-Portland, ME.

JUNE
1-Lawrence, MA.
2-Manchester, NH.
3-Concord, NH.
4-Lowell, MA.
5-Fitchburg, MA.
SUNDAY
7-Pittsfield, MA.
8-Albany, NY.
9-Troy, NY.
10-Utica, NY.
11—12-Syracuse,
  NY.
SUNDAY
14—17-Rochester,
  NY.
18-St. Catharines,
  Ont.
19-Brantford, Ont.
SUNDAY
21-Hamilton, Ont.
22—23-Toronto,
  Ont.
24-Guelph, Ont.
25-Stratford, Ont.
26-London, Ont.
SUNDAY
28—29-Detroit, MI.
30-Toledo, OH.

JULY
1-Adrian, MI.
2-Jackson, MI.
3-Lansing, MI.
SUNDAY
5-Grand Rapids, MI.
6-Kalamazoo, MI.
7-Ft. Wayne, IN.
8-Logansport, IN.
9-Lafayette, IN.
10-Danville, IL.
SUNDAY
12—17-Chicago, IL.
SUNDAY
19—24-St. Louis, MO.
SUNDAY
26-Jacksonville, IL.
27-Springfield, IL.
28-Decatur, IL.
29-Bloomington, IL.
30-Peoria, IL.
31-Galesburg, IL.

AUGUST
SUNDAY
2-Quincy, IL.
3-Keokuk, IA.
4-Burlington, IA.
5-Ottumwa, IA.
6-Oskaloosa, IA.
7-Des Moines, IA.
SUNDAY
9-Iowa Cit, IA.
10-Davenport, IA.
11-Rock Island, IL.
12-Freeport, IL.
13-Dubuque, IA.
14-Waterloo, IA.
SUNDAY
16—17-Minneapolis, MN.
18-St. Paul, MN.
19-Red Wing, MN.
20-Winona, MN.
21-LaCrosse, WI.
SUNDAY
23-Madison, WI.
24-Janesville, WI.
25-Fond du Lac, WI.
26-Oshkosh, WI.
27—28-Milwaukee, WI.
SUNDAY
30-Rockford, IL.
31-Dixon, IL.

SEPTEMBER
1-Clinton, IA.
2-Cedar Rapids, IA.
3-Marshalltown, IA.
4-Boone, IA.
SUNDAY
6-Omaha, NE; 7-Council Bluffs, IA; 8—9-St. Joseph, MO. (all dates lost because of railroad washouts)
10-Kansas City, MO.
11-Moberly, MO.
SUNDAY
13—15-St. Louis, MO.
16-Belleville, IL.
17-Carmi, IL.
18-Evansville, IN.
SUNDAY
20-Vincennes, IN.
21-Terre Haute, IN.
22—23-Indianapolis, IN.
24—25-Louisville, KY.
SUNDAY
27—30-Cincinnati, OH.

OCTOBER
1-Richmond, IN.
2-Dayton, OH.
SUNDAY
4-Columbus, OH.
5-Mt. Vernon, OH.
6-Akron, OH.
7—9-Cleveland, OH.

BIBLIOGRAPHY

BOOKS

Bailey, James M. *Life in Danbury*. Boston: 1873.

Barnum, P. T. (A. H. Saxon, editor). *Selected Letters of P. T. Barnum*. New York: Columbia University Press, 1982.

_____. *Struggles and Triumphs: or, The Life of P. T. Barnum*, Buffalo: Warren, Johnson & Co., 1872.

_____. *Struggles and Triumphs: or, The Life of P. T. Barnum*, Vol. II. New York: Alfred A. Knopf, 1927.

_____. *Struggles and Triumphs*. Buffalo: 1871.

Benton, Joel. *Life of Hon. Phineas T. Barnum*. Edgewood Publishing Company, 1891.

Conklin, George. *The Ways of the Circus*. New York: Harper & Brothers, 1921.

Coup, W. C. *Sawdust and Spangles*. Chicago: 1901.

Cumming, John. *Runners and Walkers, a Nineteenth Century Sports Chronicle*. Chicago: Regnery Gateway, 1981.

Day, Charles H. *Ink from a Circus Press Agent*. San Bernardino: The Borgo Press, 1995.

Harris, Neil. *Humbug: the Art of P. T. Barnum*. Boston: Little, Brown, 1973.

Kuhnhardt, Philip B., Jr., Philip B. III, and Peter W. Kuhnhardt, *P. T Barnum*. New York: Alfred Knopf, 1995.

Sanger, Lord George. *Seventy Years a Showman*. London: MacGibbon & Kee, 1910.

Saxon, Arthur H. *P. T. Barnum: the Legend and the Man*. New York: Columbia University Press, 1989.

ARTICLES

Bernard, Charles, "Old-Time Showmen," *Billboard*, December 31, 1932.

Crosby, J. Fred, "The Early Days of Barnum's 'Greatest on Earth,'" *Billboard*, January 21, 1922.

Dahlinger, Fred, Jr., "The Development of the Railroad Circus," *Bandwagon*, November/December, 1983; January/February, 1984.

Dunn, Pat, "Souvenir Tells Own Story of Racine's Past," Racine *Journal-Times*, June, 23, 1953.
Holland, George F., "A Long Lifetime With a Circus," *The Show World*, December 24, 1910.
Kunzog, John C., "Barnum Show Balloon Wedding," *Bandwagon*, May/June, 1964.
Loeffler, Robert J. An analysis of newspaper reports to determine the actual number of cars in Barnum's 1872 train. *White Tops*, May/June, 1983.
_____, "A Re-Examination of the History of Madison Square Garden and the Role Played by the Ringlings in the History and Air Conditioning of the Garden," Part One, *Bandwagon*, March/April, 1973.
"Nestor of Clowns, A," clipping, Syracuse (NY) *Standard*, (n.d., n.p.n.), 1899.
Pfening III, Fred D., "The Frontier and the Circus," *Bandwagon*, September/October, 1971.
"P. T. Barnum of Connecticut," copy of article by C. C. Sturtevant in Chindahl Papers, Circus-World Museum, Baraboo, Wisconsin.
Saxon, A. H., "A Franconi in America: The New York Hippodrome of 1853," *Bandwagon*, September/October, 1975.
Sturtevant, C. C., "P. T. Barnum of Connecticut," copy of article in Chindahl Papers, Circus-World Museum, Baraboo, Wisconsin.
Thayer, Stuart, "Joseph E. Warner: Pioneer of the Three Tent Circus," *Bandwagon*, January/February, 1970.
"True Origin of the Show," New York *Clipper*, May 16, 1891.
White, C. H., "More Early Circus Memories," *Bandwagon*, August 15, 1944, p. 5; December 15, 1944, p. 11.
Yadon, W. Gordon, "Barnum," *White Tops*, March/April, 1970.
_____, "Daniel A. Castello," *Banner Line*, March 15, 1968.
_____, "RBBB Actual Formation," *Banner Line*, March 15, 1968.

PERIODICALS

Akron (OH) *Daily Beacon*; Baltimore (MD) *American and Commercial Advertiser*; Boston (MA) *Dailey Globe, Evening Transcript, Journal, The Ploughman*; Buffalo (NY) *Daily Courier*; Chicago (IL) *Inter-Ocean*; Cincinnati (OH) *Enquirer*; Cleveland (OH) *Plain Dealer*; Dover (ME) *Inquirer*; Dubuque (IA)

Herald; Elizabeth (NJ) *Journal;* Evansville (IN) *Journal;* Exeter (NH) *News-Letter;* *Harper's Weekly;* Janesville (WI) *City Times;* LaCrosse (WI) *Republican and Leader;* Manchester *Daily Union;* Milwaukee (WI) *Commercial Times;* Newark (NJ) *Daily Advertiser;* New York *Clipper, Times, Tribune;* Philadelphia (PA) *Evening Bulletin, Public Record;* Pittsburgh (PA) *Daily Gazette;* Portland (ME) *Daily Press, Journal;* Portsmouth (NH) *Daily Evening Times, Journal;* Racine (WI) *Journal-Times;* Rochester (NY) *Daily Union and Advertiser;* St. Louis (MO) *Globe-Democrat;* Toledo (OH) *Blade.*

MISCELLANEOUS

Delavan Wisconsin Circus Historical Souvenir Magazine, n. p., 1970.

Dingess, John. Unpublished observations of the circus world as he knew it, generally referred to as the "Dingess manuscript." Originally a hand written document housed at the Hertzberg Collection, San Antonio Public Library, a typed copy, used here, exists in the Robert L. Parkinson Library and Research Center, Circus World Museum, Baraboo, WI.

Ludwig, Ronald V., "'Goodness Gracious' Grady's Unprecedented Old Fashioned American Circus," unpublished paper, Robert L. Parkinson Library and Research Center, Circus World Museum, Baraboo, WI.

P. T. Barnum Advance Courier for 1871, 1872, 1874, 1875.

P. T. Barnum Route Book, 1872, Circus World Museum collection.

INDEX

Admiral Dot, 18, 37, 42
Agricultural Hall, London, 72
Albino children, 107
Albino family, 37
Alhambra, 77
Alligator, 129
Ambler, Harry, 17
American Institute, 70
American Museum, 72
America's Racing Association, 138-142, 149
Anderssen, Capt., 150
Antonio, Wash, 39
Arnaud, Mon., 88, 108
Astley's Royal Amphitheatre, 76
Avery, George F., 109
Babcock, Stephen S., 9
Bailey, George F., 155, 163
Bailey, James M., 30
Baird, Howell & Co., 121
Baker, H. M., 154
Baker, Joseph, 35
Barnes, D. B., 13, 14, 17
Barnum, Bailey & Hutchinson, 163
Barnum, Mrs. P. T., 121
Barnum, P. T., 1, 5, 6, 13, 14, 15, 16, 17, 18, 22, 23, 24, 25, 26, 28, 31, 33, 34, 35, 37, 38, 39, 43, 65, 69, 70, 71, 72, 75, 80, 83, 85, 88, 89, 93, 94, 95, 97, 101, 103, 105, 109, 116, 119, 121, 123, 126, 135, 138, 141, 142, 146, 154, 155, 156, 159, 160, 161, 162, 163
Barnum's Museum Collection & VanAmburgh's Great Menagerie, 5
Barnum's Universal Exposition Company, 138, 155

Bartlett, F. A., 83
Bates, 70
Batty, William, 80
Beckwith, Alanson, 152
Bennett, Lewis, 89
Benton (boat), 10
Bernard, Charles, 81
Berry, Dr. A. C., 18, 35
Bishop, George, 9
Bismarck, 85
Black Eagle, Captain of La Crosse, 126
Blondin, 91
Bluebeard, 130, 131, 133, 143
Bronze Horse, The, 76
Buckley circus, 2
Buckley, E. C., 126
Buckley, Edward, 9, 17, 35, 123
Buckley, Harriet, 17
Buckley, Harry, 6, 13, 14, 17, 35, 121, 123, 125
Buckley, Marienne, 123
Buckley, Matthew, 35, 123
Buckley, Page, 35, 123
Buckley, Soulier & Co.'s Hippodrome, 123
Buckley's National Circus, 2
Bunnell brothers, 37, 107
Burke, Mr., 112
Burr Robbins' Circus, 121
Bushnell, George, 17
Butler, George B., 71
Butler, L. G., 6
California Menagerie, 75
Car of Neptune, 24
Car of the Muses, 24
Cardiff giant, 19
Castello & VanVleck's Mammoth Circus, 3

178

Castello show, 17
Castello, Dan, 1, 2, 3, 5, 6, 7, 10, 13, 15, 17, 18, 23, 25, 33, 34, 38, 72, 75, 77, 80, 83, 129, 154, 159, 160, 161, 163
Castello, Dan Jr., 2, 9, 10
Castello, Dave, 25
Castello, Frances, 2, 3, 9, 33
Castello, Howes & Nixon, 5
Castello, Mrs. Dan, 2, 3, 9, 25, 33
Castello, Harry, 25
Castello, Johnny, 25
Castello's Circus & Egyptian Caravan, 1, 7, 14
Castello's Great Show, 3, 5
Castineyra, Alice, 99, 108, 113
Central Park Zoo, 103
Chandler, Mr., 112
Chariot of Orpheus, 23
Chase for a Wife, 89
Cinderella, 76, 77, 146
Circassian girl, 149
Circus Renz, Vienna, 71
Clarke, Kit, 46
Clemens, Samuel, 101, 135
Codington, 70
Cole, W. W., 155
Colton, Charles S., 118
Colvin, E. D., 155
Confucious, 86
Congress of Nations, The, 65, 72, 83, 91, 103, 105, 107, 108, 127, 133, 139, 141, 143, 147
Conklin, George, 163
Conklin, Pete, 3, 14
Conklin, Theodore, 26
Conrad, William, 131
Cook, Mary Irene, 115
Cook, W. I., 115
Cooke, Henry Welby, 131
Cooke, Louis E., 75
Cooke's Equestrian Troupe, 76
Cooke's Royal Circus, 75
Cooper, James E., 35

Cotton, Mary, 113
Coup, George, 35
Coup, Mrs. W. C., 6
Coup, W. C., 1, 6, 9, 11, 13, 14, 15, 16, 17, 18, 22, 23, 25, 26, 33, 34, 35, 38, 42, 43, 46, 69, 72, 83, 86, 101, 103, 119, 126, 132, 146, 153, 154, 159, 160, 161, 162
Crane & Co.'s Great Oriental Circus, 76
Cremorne Gardens, London, 77
Crum, W. C., 17, 35, 126
Cumiski, 70
D'Atalie, Mme., 88, 108, 133, 143
Dan Rice's Paris Pavilion Circus, 30, 75
DaVinci, Carlotta, 25
Davis, Annie, 99
Day, Charles H., 159, 161
Deerfoot, 89
DeHaven, George W., 3, 102, 138
Delaney, Frank, 17
Denier, John, 91
Dickens, Charles, 3
Dingess, Robert, 126
Dockrill, Mme., 134
Donaldson, David L., 95
Donaldson, Frances, 9, 11
Donaldson, Prof. W. H., 94, 95, 96, 97, 101, 108, 109, 112, 113, 115, 118, 121, 147, 148, 149, 150, 152, 153, 155
Donnybrook Fair; or, The Lancaster Races, 91, 141
Dutton, William, 25
Dyer, Edward, 26
Eagan, William H., 95
Eastlake, Tom (Miaco), 9
Edge, Mr., 112
Edward the Black Prince, 85
Elixir of Life, or, the Birth of Harlequin, The, 77
Ellsler, Fanny, 83

179

Emerson, Rev. G. H., 28
Evans, John, 138
Fairy Prince O'Donohue, The, 77
Fellows, 70
Fete at Pekin, The, 127, 131, 134, 141, 143
Field of the Cloth of Gold, The, 76
Fiji cannibals, 37
Fish Brothers Wagon Co., 13, 17
Fish, Charles, 38
Fish, Nancy (2nd Mrs. Barnum), 119
Fisher, Mr., 112
Flatfoots, 163
Ford, Gordon L., 69
Forepaugh circus, 126
Forepaugh, Adam, 24
Fox, C. J., 115
Franconi, Henri, 66
Franconi, Victor, 80
Franconi's Hippodrome, 66, 75
Franklin, John, 34
Frost, Hyatt, 155
Fuller, Charles W., 75, 129
Fulton, E. P. Jr., 115
George W. DeHaven's Circus, 102
Gilbert, Harry, 118
Gilchrist Transportation Company, 10
Gildersleeve, W. May, 9
Gilmore, P. S., 134
Girardeau, Maria Celeste, 25
Glenroy, John, 3
Golden Egg, The, 77
Goliath, Mons., 29
Gonzalez, Pedro (Dan Castello), 2
Grady, Ella, 91, 113
Grady, G. G., 99
Grady's Old Fashioned American Circus, 99, 102, 121
Grant, Ulysses S., 15
Great Chicago Circus, 102
Great Novelty Railroad Circus, 102

Greeley, Horace, 15
Grimwood, N. S., 150, 152
Gymnastic Tournament, 93
Haight & Co.'s Great Eastern, 121, 138
Haight & Co.'s Great Southern, 121, 138
Haight, Andrew, 138
Hall, George W. Jr., 123
Hardenberger & Co.'s Circus, 163
Harlequin Bluebeard, 77
Harlequin Mother Goose, 77
Hartman, Prof. Fritz, 35, 107
Hawley, David R., 9, 25
Hayden, Prof. J. W., 102
Hengler's Circus, 3
Henry, Joseph, 80
Herbert, Mr., 112
Higgins tent makers, 147
Higgins, Frank, 116
Hindley, Pauline, 25
Hippocampus (boat), 10
Hippodrome, Paris, 71
Hogle, 108, 133
Howes & Castello's Great Circus, 5
Howes & Cushing's American Circus, 3
Howes, Egbert, 5, 155
Howes, Seth B., 5, 65
Howes' Globe telescoper, 14
Howes' Great European, 5
Howes' Great London, 35, 42, 121, 134
Hoyle, William, 91
Hudson's (J. M.) Circus, 102
Hungerford, James, 115
Hurd, Helen (nee Barnum), 72
Hurd, S. H., 18, 34, 69, 72, 83, 136, 153, 154, 159
Hutchinson, J. L., 17, 35, 44
Il Re Galantuomo, 85
Indian Life, 141
Indian Mazeppa, The, 90

J. E. Warner's Great Pacific, 19
Jackley Family, 129, 130
Jackley, Nathan, 134
Jackley's Vienna Circus, 134
Jackson, Mr., 152
James Robinson's Circus, 102
January act, 7
Janvier, Mr., 111
Jeannette Roberts (boat), 5
Jeffries, Rev., 118
Joan of Arc, 126
Johnson, Mr., 111
Joignerey, Mons., 88
Joseph, Sam H., 138
Jukes, W. L., 17
June & Co., 80
June & Turner Circus, 2
June, Lewis, 163
Justice, J. J., 17, 25
Kellogg, B. S., 83
Kennebel Brothers, 129
Kennebel, Eugene, 134
Kennebel, François, 134
Kennebel, Joseph, 134
Kimball, Moses, 15
King William of German, 19
King, Samuel A., 152
Kreps, 70
Ku Klux Klan skit, 9
Lake, Agnes, 102
Lake's Hippo-Olympiad, 102
Lazelle, 108
Lazelle and Millson, 38, 39, 133
Leake, Anna E., 37
Lee, Gus, 39
Lee, H. C., 80
Lengel, Elijah, 5
Lent, L. B., 34, 38, 75, 131
Lent's New York Circus, 102, 131
Leon, Signor, 88
Leonchi, 90
Leonchi's Tribe of Indians, 89
Leslie, Harry, 91
Lewis, Mattie, 91, 95, 129, 143

Lewis, Miss, 108
Lewis, Owen, 95
Ling Look, 129, 134
Little All Right, 90, 129, 133
Louis Napoleon, 19
Loyal, Mons., 88, 108
Lusbie, Ben, 35
Mabie Bros., 2, 6
Madden, George, 17, 39
Madden, Mary Anne, 17
Madison Square Garden, 134
Maginley, Ben, 155
Major Brown's circus, 2
March of the Monarchs, The, 107
Marion Sisters, 25
Marquesas Cannibals, 126
Mason, Mary, 99, 121
McClean, Charles H., 147
McIntyre, E., 95
Mechanics Pavilion, 66
Melville, Alex, 39
Melville, Frank, 39, 131
Melville, George, 25, 39
Melville, James, 38, 131, 155
Merry Sports of England, 76
Miaco, Hawley & Rivers, 10
Miaco, Tom, 9, 25
Miles, R. E. J., 102, 138
Millson, 108
Millson & Lazelle, 88
Millson, Fanny, 113
Moltke, Gen., 19
Monitor Show, 75
Monte Verde, 39
Montgomery Queen Circus, 121
Morgan, Mr., 112
Morrison, John, 10
Mullen, Edward, 96
Murray, John, 155
Myers, James W., 75
Myers' Circus, Dresden, 71
Napoleon I, 85
Napoleon III, 91
Nathans, Estell, 9

Nathans, J. J., 155, 163
Nathans, Philo, 9
New National Circus, 76
New York and Harlem Railroad Company, 70
New York Central Park Zoo, 130
Niblo's Garden, 76, 93, 127
Nixon & Co., 2
Nixon & Kemp, 75
Nixon, James M., 3, 5, 6, 75, 77, 83, 93, 107, 133, 134
North, George, 91, 108, 133
North, Levi J., 80, 155
Noyes' Crescent City Circus, 102
O'Brien's Caravan, Monster Menagerie and National Kingdom, 163
O'Brien, John, 130, 162
Older & Chandler, 102
Oriental Festival, The, 77
Orpheus bandwagon, 42
Oswald, Maud, 99, 108
Painter & Durand, 66
Palace Gardens, NYC, 77
Palmer, Henry D., 155
Payne, C. N., 97
Pedanto, Signor, 112
Pell, Charles C., 35
Pierce, W. E., 10
Pond, J. B., 18
"Pony Races, The", 76
Primey, A. C., 95
P. T. Barnum (balloon), 105, 109, 153
P. T. Barnum Universal Exposition Company, 101
P. T. Barnum's New York Prototype Hippodrome, 123
Queen Isabella, 86
Queen Victoria, 85
Rankin, 70
Rasmussen, Mr., 150
Ravel, Marietta, 91
Reiche Brothers, 18

Revolving Temple of Juno, 24
Reynolds III, Richard J., 129
Rice, Dan, 30, 80, 138
Rivers, 9
Rivers & Derious, 75, 121
Robinson, James, 38
Robinson, John, 39, 118, 155
Robinson, Stump, 35
Robinson, Yankee, 126
Robinson's Circus, 2, 39
Rosinski Troupe, 134
Runnells, Bonnie, 25
Runnells, Burnell, 25
Runnells, Freddie, 25
Salesday at Tattersall, or, Scenes Among the English Turfmen, 132
Salinyea Brothers, 9
Sands, Richard, 65
Sanger, George, 72
Sanger, John, 72
Sarah Van Eps (boat), 9
Satsuma, 90, 129, 133
Satterlee-Bell and Co., 2
Saulsbury, Miss, 108
Saunders, John, 9, 11
Savage, George, 115
Seymour, Carrie, 127, 143
Sheldenberger's European Menagerie and Grecian Circus, 163
Shield of the Cloth of Gold, The, 77
Siamese twins, 19
Silamonski and Carré's Circus, Cologne, 71
Sloman, George, 17
Smith, Avery, 65, 155, 163
Smith, George W., 127
Smith, James, 126
Smith, Prof. George, 143
Smith, Richard, 112
Smith, Washington, 17
Smith, William, 17

Soulier, Mons., 126
Spalding & Rogers, 2, 3
Spalding, Gilbert R., 34
Spencer, J. M., 147
Spirit of the Flood, 77
Sprites of the Silvery Shower, 25
Standish, Sargeant, 126
Stark, John H., 95
Steeple-Chase; or Life in Merry England, The, 77
Stevens, 108, 133
Stevens & Begun, 121
Stevens, Benjamin, 91
Stewart, A. A., 155
Stickney & Son, 121
Stickney, Bob, 39
Stowe, Harriet Beecher, 15
Stowe's Great Western, 121
Stroup, J. C., 116
Summerfield, 29
Taylor, Maggie, 113, 118, 119
Temple of Juno, 42
Terrace Garden Theatre, 131
Thayer's (James L.) Circus, 102
Thomas, D. S., 44, 75, 106, 116, 118, 153
Thompson, Corporal, 66
Thornell, 70
Thumb, Tom, 119
Tilden, Luke, 17, 35
Titus, Lewis B., 65
Tree, Ellen, 83
Tryon, John, 76
Turner, Aaron, 76
Upp, Prof. Max, 126
VanAmburgh & Co., 5
VanAmburgh Menagerie, 24
Vanderbilt, William H., 86
Van Houghton Circus, 121
Van Houghton, W., 126
VanValkenberg, Richard, 3
Victoria, Mlle., 90, 91, 95, 108, 121

View of Donnybrook Fair, 131
Vienna International Exhibition, 69, 85
Virginie, Mlle., 9
Von Moltke, 85
Waldon, Mlle., 126
Walsh, Mary, 99, 108, 118
Warner & Co.'s Great Pacific Menagerie and Circus, 163
Warren & Henderson, 121
Warren, Lavinia, 119
Waterman, Walter, 155
Watson, Tom, 131
Welch, Rufus, 80
Welsh, Tommy, 26
Westendorf, Bob, 17
Weston, Edward Payson, 96
"What Is It?", 149
Wheeler, S. O., 75
White, Charles, 25, 35, 38, 90, 111
Whittaker, Frank, 83, 118
Wild, W., 95
Wilhelm, 85, 86
William the Conqueror, 85
Wilson, John, 66
Wilson's Hippodrome, San Francisco, 66
Wizard Skiff, The, 77
Wood, George, 17, 18, 19
Woods, L. B., 83
Wootten & Andrews, 121
Wootten & Haight's Empire City Circus, 102
Yadon, W. Gordon, 13
Yamadiva, 129
Yankee Robinson circus, 6
Yates, Annie, 99, 108, 119
Zanfretta, Mlle., 91
Zip, 107
Zoölogical Gardens, Hamburg, 72
Zoological Gardens, London, 91
Zoyara, Ella, 66

www.ingramcontent.com/pod-product-compliance
Lightning Source LLC
Chambersburg PA
CBHW032115090426
42743CB00007B/364